VOLCANOES

OF THE WORLD

BILL MCGUIRE
CHRISTOPHER KILBURN

THUNDER BAY
P·R·E·S·S

R G W

COVER AND RIGHT: Mount St. Helens
© 1995 COMSTOCK, INC.

This edition published in 1997 by
Thunder Bay Press
5880 Oberlin Drive, Suite 400
San Diego, California 92121-9653
1-800-284-3580

http:/www.adms.web.com

Produced by the
Promotional Reprint Company Ltd,
Kiln House, 210 New Kings Road, London SW6 4NZ

Copyright © 1997 Promotional Reprint Company Ltd

Library of Congress Cataloging
in Publication Data available upon request.

ISBN 1 57145 079 3

Printed and bound in China

1 2 3 4 5 97 98 99 00 01

The Publisher would like to thank all the individuals and
organizations that supplied illustrations for use in this book;
in particular we'd like to thank Jacques Durieux for the emotive descriptions
of his work and the photographs on pages 52-63 and 72-83.

A. Aparicio: 141 (bottom)

A.P. Jones: 45 (top), 47 (both), 117 (both), 120, 122 (top and center), 123 (top)

C. Monteath/Mountain Camera: 90, 91 (both), 92/93

C. Solana: 108, 109, 110, 111

C.R.J. Kilburn: 6, 15, 17, 27 (top), 28/29, 30, 31, 34 (bottom), 101, 139 (bottom)

Comstock Inc, London: Cover, 1, 3

D.C. Munro: 140 (top)

D.P. Hill: 96

G. Filton: 45 (bottom)

H. Pinkerton: 18/19, 48, 49, 51, 137 (both), 143 (both)

I. Cleare/Mountain Camera:

55 (both), 56/57, 58, 58/59, 60/61, 62, 63, 72, 73, 74 (both), 75, 76/77, 78 (all), 79, 80, 81 (all), 82 (all), 83 (all)

L. Gurioli: 33 (bottom)

M. Dickinson/Mountain Camera: 121 (bottom), 122 (bottom), 123 (bottom)

P. Fidczuk: 35

P. Harper/Mountain Camera: 121 (top)

Pictor International — London: 67 (top), 69, 102/103, 106/107, 127, 132/133

S. Helano da Silva: 142

T.N. Gautier: 97, 98/99

USGS: 23, 139 (top)

W.I. McGuire: 5, 10 (both).

17,99

CONTENTS

INTRODUCTION

Ever since our distant ancestors roamed the Earth, volcanoes have been feared and respected for the death and destruction they bring. At the same time, however, they have brought life, both to the planet itself and to the increasing numbers of people who inhabit their slopes. Since the end of the ice age around 10,000 years ago, over 1,500 volcanoes have erupted — some many times over — wreaking havoc on a local, regional, and occasionally global scale. It has been estimated that over one million people have died as a result of volcanic activity over the past 2000 years, including a quarter of a million people since the start of the 18th century, and around 60,000 since 1900. More recently, the high-profile eruption of

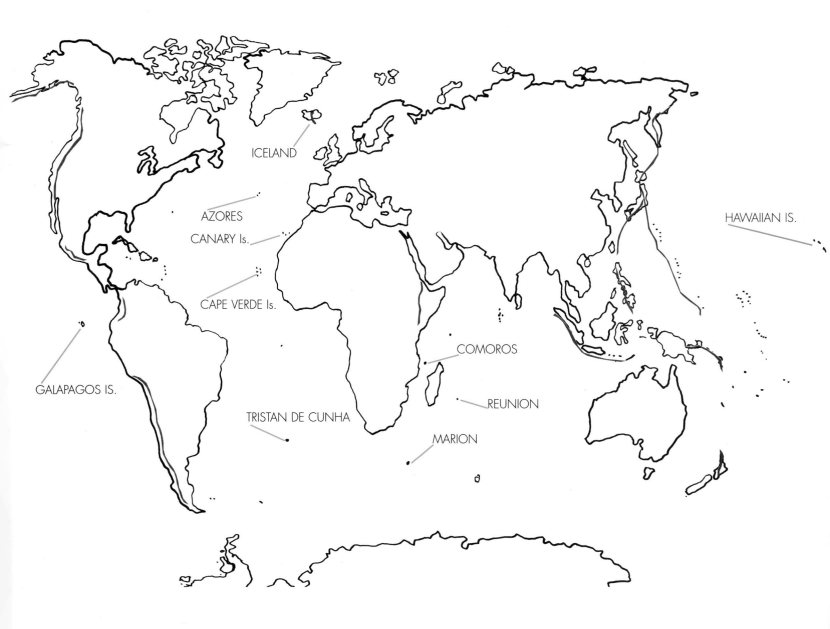

ICELAND

AZORES
CANARY Is.

CAPE VERDE Is.

HAWAIIAN IS.

COMOROS

GALAPAGOS IS.

REUNION

TRISTAN DE CUNHA

MARION

INTRODUCTION

Mount St. Helens (Washington State, USA) during May 1980 heralded the worst series of volcanic disasters since the early years of the century, with over 30,000 killed since then. Between 1980 and 1990 alone, nearly two thirds of a million lives have been seriously affected by volcanic activity, almost all in the developing world.

As well as death, however, volcanoes also bring life. During the early history of the Earth, gases issuing from the interior of the planet via countless volcanic vents led to the creation of both the atmosphere and the oceans, on which all life depends for its existence. Some of the most fertile soils are also derived from the breakdown of volcanic products, while in many parts of the world the solidified lavas themselves are used for building purposes. Volcanoes are also an immense source of cheap power, and in Iceland volcanically-derived hydrothermal power heats the glass houses which keep the population in fresh fruit and vegetables. Volcanic scenery is often spectacular and in many parts of the world attracts the tourist. The volcanoes of Iceland, Hawaii, New Zealand, and the Canary Islands (Spain), the Aegean volcanic island of Santorini, and Vesuvius — the destroyer of Pompeii — accrue major economic benefits to their regions through the attraction of large numbers of tourists. Where volcanoes are high enough and cold enough, such as Ruapehu (New Zealand), Mount Etna (Sicily), and Mammoth Lakes (California) they even support ski resorts which underpin the entire local economy.

Currently around ten percent of the world's population lives close to an active or dormant volcano, a number which is certain to rise dramatically as we enter the new millenium. Most volcanoes are located in poor, developing world countries with rapidly-growing populations, strong competition for agricultural land, and limited resources. Despite the dangers they pose, volcanoes are often viewed as saviours, providing sought-after living space, rich soils for farming, and valuable materials for building. In many cases, a volcano has not erupted in living memory so the local population has little inkling of the threat which hangs over them. Compounding this problem is the fact that many developing world volcanoes have only been poorly studied, and may not be monitored at all. This is typically the result of a combination of factors, including the lack of suitable scientific and technical expertise, limited financial resources, and the absence of political incentive.

Throughout the 1990s, as part of the United Nations International Decade for Natural Disaster Reduction (IDNDR), volcanologists from around the world have dedicated themselves to learning more about the world's 600 or so active volcanoes, with the aim of reducing the numbers of volcanic disasters in an increasingly populous world. This initiative has involved monitoring greater

A river of molten lava flowing down the flanks of Mt Etna. The active river in yellow has a temperature of about 1,100°C (2,012°F). The dark banks are made from earlier lava that has solidified, but whose interiors are still at temperatures of several hundreds of degrees centigrade.

numbers of volcanoes, only about a fifth of which are currently under surveillance, studying the products of past activity to make better forecasts about the nature of future eruptions, and educating and training the civil authorities and inhabitants of volcanic regions. As we enter the new millenium it is hoped that as a result of this work the numbers of volcanic eruptions leading to volcanic disasters will be dramatically reduced.

WHERE TO FIND VOLCANOES

Volcanoes are not designed to threaten humanity. They exist because the Earth has been losing heat since its formation 4,600 million years ago. Under the combined influence of cooling and gravity, our planet has evolved a basic threefold structure, topped by the atmosphere and oceans: a spherical core of iron from the centre of the Earth (6,400km/4,000 miles deep) to depths of 2,900km (1,800 miles); an intermediate mantle of silicate rock (rich also in heavy elements such as iron and magnesium) about 2,800km (1,700 miles) thick; and an outer crust (more silicate rock, but richer than the mantle in lighter elements such as sodium and potassium), with an average thickness of about 40km (25 miles) beneath the continents and 5km (3 miles) below the oceans.

Most of the Earth is solid because the melting temperature of rock increases with depth, as the rock is put under greater pressure by the weight of material above. Though the Earth also becomes hotter inwards (reaching over 6,000°C/11,000°F at its centre), the increase in pressure prevents melting near the surface except for a narrow range of depths between about 30 and 200km (20–120 miles). This does not mean that the crust is sitting on an underground lake of molten rock, or magma. Rather, it rests on a mushy zone which, if sufficiently disturbed by some other factor, can produce localised pockets of magma. Volcanoes simply mark where magma has penetrated the crust after a disturbance has occurred.

A cursory glance at the world map shows that volcanoes are not randomly distributed, but occur mainly along well-defined chains, hundreds to thousands of kilometres long. Particularly clear are the chains around the Pacific Ocean (from Chile to Alaska, across to Kamchatka, Japan, the Philippines, Indonesia and New Zealand), in the Caribbean, through Europe's Mediterranean countries, and along the eastern half of the African continent. Beneath the oceans, too, volcanic ridges run down the middle of the Atlantic, through the Indian Ocean and around the rim of Antarctica. The whole planet, it seems, is crossed by a network of volcanoes, as if the Earth's surface were broken china letting magma leak through the cracks.

Where the crust fails is strongly influenced by movements in the mantle. To lose its heat most efficiently, the Earth has estab-

The snow-capped peak of Mt Ruapehu, the highest point on the North Island of New Zealand. In 1953, a mudflow from the volcano destroyed a bridge carrying the Wellington-Auckland express train, killing over 150 people.

lished very slow circulation (or convection) patterns within its interior, much like the large patterns known to drive ocean currents. Creeping at a few centimetres a year (about the speed at which fingernails grow), the mantle tries to drag the crust along with it. The convective patterns, however, do not move all in the same direction, so that while some parts of the crust are being stretched sideways, others are being squeezed together.

The crust has responded by arranging itself into about a dozen large plates and by concentrating deformation along their margins. The plates move relative to each other and, as might be expected, they can behave in four ways (the essence of Plate Tectonics): they can tear away from each other, allowing new material to well-up from below and to generate new crust (constructive plate margins); they can collide to crumple, thicken the crust and create mountain ranges (such as the Alps and Himalayas); they can collide so that one plate is forced beneath another (subduction zones); or they can slide past each other laterally (such as along California's San Andreas fault).

Most active volcanoes are found at constructive plate margins (where crustal tearing allows the easy escape of magma) or subduction zones (where melting is triggered by burial of the subducted plate margin). All ocean ridges are constructive margins (the floor of the Atlantic, for example, is spreading about 2cm (0.8in) a year east and west from its central ridge) and volcanic rift systems are often linked to the stretching of crust before a new plate margin is formed or the attempt is aborted; most volcanoes on land are associated with subduction, the leading example being the Pacific volcanic chains, caused by subduction of the Pacific floor beneath the American, Eurasian, and Australian plates. Notable exceptions are the few volcanoes found isolated in the heart of a plate (eg, Emi Koussi in Chad, north-central Africa; Kunlun in Western China; or the Hawaiian Islands in the Pacific). Some of these, at least, seem to overlie subsidiary currents (or plumes) of upwelling mantle, divorced from the currents below plate margins, although the details of their behaviour are still a matter of debate.

HOW VOLCANOES WORK

Molten rock is less dense than when it is solid. Once a suitably large volume has been melted underground, the buoyancy of the new magma becomes great enough to force a pathway upwards through the rock overhead. The speed of ascent is normally uneven, short periods of rapid movement being interrupted by long intervals at almost a standstill. Thousands of years or more may pass between melting and eruption.

Magma is a mixture of mainly eight elements: oxygen, silicon,

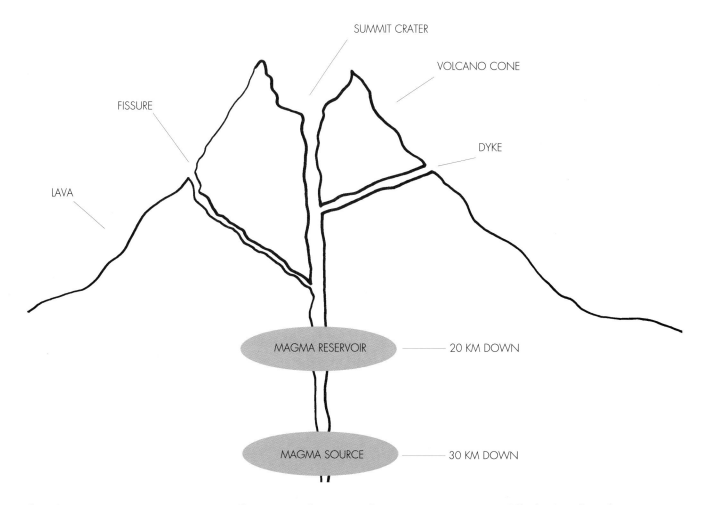

SUMMIT CRATER

VOLCANO CONE

FISSURE

DYKE

LAVA

MAGMA RESERVOIR — 20 KM DOWN

MAGMA SOURCE — 30 KM DOWN

aluminum, iron, magnesium, calcium, sodium, and potassium. As it rises, the mixture meets cooler rocks and begins once more to solidify. The first crystals to appear are rich in those elements with high melting points (iron and magnesium), but poor in those with lower melting points, such as sodium and potassium. Later crystals have different compositions, according to the elements left in the remaining magmatic liquid, so that both newly-forming crystals and remaining liquid change in composition as solidification proceeds. Some crystals get left behind either as they grow onto the rock around the magma or because they can settle slowly through the remaining liquid. By the time magma reaches the surface, its composition may be quite different from that when it first formed, the greater changes occurring among magmas that take longer to ascend.

Dozens of names are needed to distinguish in detail the world's volcanic rocks. Fortunately, however, only four names are essential to describe the vast majority. In order of increasing amounts of crystallization before eruption (ie, the more rapidly-ascending magmas first), they are basalt, andesite, dacite, and rhyolite. Rich in iron and magnesium, basalts are black and, though common throughout the world, they are most often found at volcanoes where the crust is splitting apart (since magma can ascend more rapidly; for this rea-

The basics of a volcano: magma rises to the surface to erupt. The effects of an eruption are shown on page 17.

ABOVE: Collapse of a growing lava dome on Montserrat Island in the Caribbean during the summer of 1996. Falling blocks of lava are disintegrating into fine dust, forming a pyroclastic flow at about 400°C (750°F).

RIGHT: Mudflows burying houses on the flanks of Mt. Pinatubo in the Philippines, after its cataclysmic eruption in 1991. The mudflows, or lahars, are produced during heavy storms, as rain washes loose ash from the upper flanks of the volcano.

FAR RIGHT: Layers of volcanic ash cover the Governor's residence and surrounding houses in Plymouth, the evacuated capital of Montserrat. Much of the ash was deposited after an explosive eruption on 17 September 1996.

OVERLEAF: Collecting samples from flowing lava on Mt. Etna. The protective suit is necessary to resist the heat from the lava at about 1,100°C (2,012°F).

son, the ocean floors are basaltic). Dacites and rhyolites are grey-white (potassium, sodium, silicon, and oxygen favour pale-coloured solids) and occur mostly at volcanoes above subduction zones, because the process of subduction, though enhancing melting at depth, involves compression of the crust and so slows the rate of magma ascent.

Magma composition is important because it controls how volcanoes erupt. All magmas contain a small amount of dissolved volatiles, most importantly water. When close to the surface, the pressure on the magma becomes low enough to let the volatiles emerge within the liquid as bubbles of gas (exactly as bubbles of carbon dioxide appear in a bottle of soda water when pressure is released by opening the top). The growth of bubbles expands the total volume of the magma, which then exerts a greater pressure on the rock around it. If the liquid is sufficiently fluid, the bubbles can escape from the magma to emerge at the surface as outpourings of gas. In this case, large pressures do not build up in the magma, which can later erupt as a lava flow (lava and magma are identical but, because of an historical quirk, the word lava became used to describe magma once it had broken the surface). At the opposite extreme, if the magmatic fluid is viscous enough to slow the migrating bubbles, they may collect to form either a small number of huge bubbles or a pressurised froth.

When a huge bubble forms and bursts at the surface, its broken skin of magma is hurled away as a collection of fragments sometimes metres across, in a so-called strombolian eruption, named after the activity common on Stromboli, a volcanic island in the Mediterranean. When a froth forms and reaches the surface, it disintegrates and erupts as a high-pressure gas carrying blobs of viscous magma. The less-violent mixtures remain as a jet, appearing from the distance as a glowing lava fountain. Jets under greater pressure typically break down the viscous magma into fine particles, or ash. Entering the atmosphere at over 800°C (1,500°F), collections of ash heat the air around them and so buoy themselves upwards as a convecting eruption column that may reach into the stratosphere, where volcanic ash and gases can remain for years, circulating the globe and upsetting the weather [eruptions producing such columns are sometimes described as plinian, after the account by Pliny the Younger of the AD 79 eruption of Vesuvius (see Personal Experiences pages 24 and 25)]. The outside layers of these columns chill more rapidly than the layers within and, mixing further with cold air, they can eventually become too cold (but still at 500°C/900°F or more) and heavy to continue being buoyed upwards. At this stage, the outer layers collapse to form clouds of ash and gas that, having crashed to the ground, are heavy enough to

RIGHT: The opening phases of explosive activity at the Northeast Crater of Mt. Etna in 1986. The billowing clouds consist of fine black ash (which shows a dirty colour) mixed with white steam.

hug the surface and race downslope at hurricane velocities. Such pyroclastic flows (or ignimbrites, once called *nuées ardentes*) are among the most terrifying of all volcanic phenomena. Beneath one of these flows, a thriving settlement can become a ghost town in less than five minutes (see pages 124–126). When the volume erupted is very large (typically a cubic kilometre at least), the surface of the volcano can founder into the gap left by the escaped magma, leaving a surface depression, or caldera, kilometres or more in diameter.

The viscosity of erupting magma increases along the crystallization sequence from basalt to rhyolite. While all these magmas have been seen to erupt as lavas (basalts at around 1,100°C/2,000°F, dacites at about 850°C/1,500°F), their common styles of explosive activity correspond to their typical fluidity upon eruption: hence, basaltic-to-andesitic volcanoes (eg, Etna, and Hawaii's Kilauea and Mauna Loa) are associated with strombolian explosions and lava fountains, whereas andesitic-to-rhyolitic volcanoes (eg, Mount St. Helens, Pinatubo and Novarupta) are linked with sustained eruption columns and pyroclastic flows. Styles of volcanic eruption are thus closely tied both to particular types of plate margin and to their own peculiar sets of hazards. For this reason, studies on, say, Etna, have little direct application to Mount St. Helens, so that it is important to evaluate each hazardous volcano in turn.

VOLCANIC HAZARDS AND HOW TO COPE WITH THEM
Volcanoes are unique amongst natural hazards in the remarkable number of different ways by which they can bring death and destruction. Interestingly, the spectacular streams of red-hot lava, which most view as the epitome of volcanic activity, are the least dangerous. Of much greater concern are pyroclastic flows — clouds of molten lava droplets and incandescent volcanic gases — which travel down the flanks of explosive volcanoes at velocities in excess of 100kph (60mph), and which have killed at least 60,000 people over the past 400 years. As testified by the complete devastation of the town of St. Pierre on the Caribbean island of Martinique by the 1902 eruption of Mt Pelée, these flows are capable — within a few minutes — of razing a town to the ground and killing virtually all its inhabitants. Similarly destructive are the rivers of mud (lahars) produced when an eruption melts snow and ice or when heavy rains fall on thick deposits of loose volcanic ash. In the worst volcanic disaster since St. Pierre, lahars generated by a relatively small eruption at Nevado del Ruiz in Colombia in 1985 left over 22,000 dead as they buried the town of Armero and neighbouring settlements.

Casualties may also result from the heavy ash fall, which characteristically accompanies all explosive eruptions, causing roof collapse and breathing problems, the poisoning of livestock, and

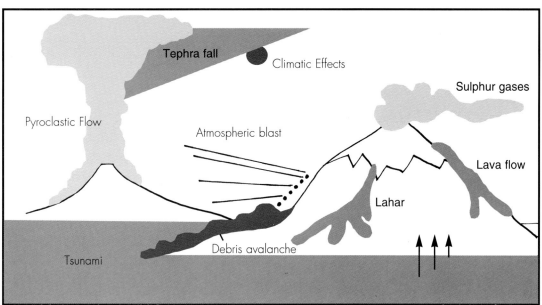

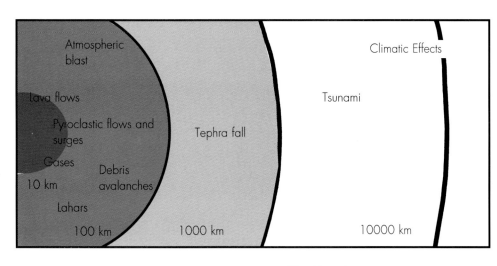

TOP: The twin peaks of Vesuvius from across the sea-filled caldera of Campi Flegrei. The photograph was taken from where Pliny the Younger watched Vesuvius erupting in AD 79.

ABOVE LEFT: The principal hazards from active volcanoes.

LEFT: The ranges of volcanic hazards.

contamination of water supplies. Other volcanic hazards result from large-scale collapse of the flanks of a volcano, triggering huge landslides, and atmospheric shock waves, and — where the collapsing material enters a body of water — potentially devastating giant waves known as tsunami.

The secondary or longer-term consequences of major volcanic eruptions have also been responsible for some of the largest volcanic catsastrophes on record. During 1783, for example, 500 million tonnes of noxious gases issuing from the Laki fissure eruption in Iceland contaminated pasture and water sources to the extent that a quarter of a million livestock died. The resulting mass starvation resulted in over 10,000 deaths — over 25% of the island's population. Similarly over 80,000 of the 92,000 deaths caused by the gigantic 1815 eruption of Tambora in Indonesia — the biggest eruption since the ice age — also resulted from famine. This eruption also affected the global climate to such an extent that the following year — 1816 — was known as the year without a summer, with winter conditions in Europe and North America even during the summer months.

Despite the devastating effects of many eruptive phenomena,

there are many ways in which these can be minimised. Hazard mapping — locating the products of previous eruptions — allows those areas likely to be threatened again by various hazardous phenomena to be identified, while continuous geophysical and geochemical monitoring can identify those signs, for example increased numbers of earthquakes, which indicate that a dormant volcano is becoming active. Damage to property can be minimised by preventing building in valleys and on low ground which is likely to be affected by pyroclastic flows and lahars, while pre-evacuation, based on information derived from monitoring and hazard mapping, can dramatically limit death and injury in the event of an impending eruption. Contingency plans for temporary refugee camps and medical facilities can also be developed, ready to be activated at short notice, along with provision for sufficient supplies of clean water, food, and adequate hygene facilities. Critically, however, reducing volcanic disasters relies most importantly on being able to communicate the nature of the problem to the civil authorities and local population, so that they respond rapidly and appropriately in the event of a volcanic crisis. The legacy of failure in this respect could be another disaster on the scale of Nevado del Ruiz.

Steam from vaporised rainwater rising above recently active lava on Hawaii.

INTRODUCTION

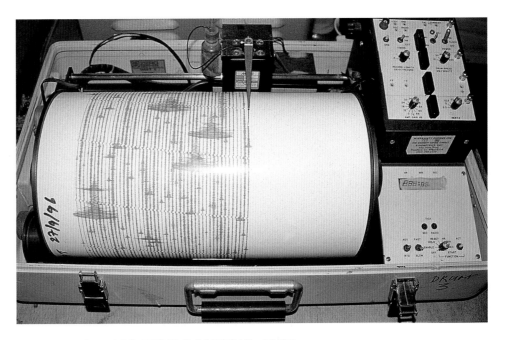

A seismograph monitoring tremors within the South Soufriere Hills volcano on Montserrat in 1996. Tremors are caused by rock fracturing, motion of magma, and by huge boulders pounding the ground as they collapse from an active lava dome. Changes in the pattern of shaking often signal a shift in the volcano's eruptive behaviour. The active lava dome can be seen in the top photograph on page 10.

MONITORING VOLCANOES AND FORECASTING ERUPTIONS

Volcanoes have been monitored, with varying degrees of success, since the first volcano observatory was established in 1847 on the slopes of Vesuvius. A monitoring programme is crucial to reducing the chances of a volcanic disaster through forecasting the timing and nature of a forthcoming eruption. Continous monitoring over a long period of time, using a range of geophysical and geochemical sensors, can establish the normal or baseline behaviour of a particular volcano. This is essential if any future anomalous activity — which might presage an eruption — is to be recognised.

For many years, seismic and ground deformation monitoring were the only techniques available to the volcanologist, and although a whole range of new methods are now available, these remain the most useful means of detecting fresh magma entering a volcano prior to eruption. Seismometers measure the micro-earthquakes associated with rock fracturing as new magma makes space for itself en route to the surface, while a range of surveying methods (including precise levelling and electronic distance measurement) detect the swelling of the volcano as fresh magma is emplaced within. These core methods are now augmented by an impressive range of newer monitoring techniques designed to measure a range of physical and chemical parameters, changes in which may mean that an eruption is on its way. These include the compositions of gases and hot springs, and the values of the local gravity, electrical, and magnetic fields. The use of satellite-borne sensors is also becoming increasingly important in volcanology, enabling the monitoring of both thermal changes and ground deformation from orbit; a facility which is particularly useful where a volcano is poorly accessible on the ground.

Even when a volcano has been monitored for a long period of time, and its baseline behaviour is well understood, forecasting the timing and nature of a future eruption is a difficult business, and remains as much an art as a science. This is especially the case where there has been no eruption in living memory. Once a volcano has become activated and fresh magma has been detected entering the volcano, a number of particular forecasting problems arise. These include deciding whether the new magma is actually going to trigger an eruption at all, or whether it is simply going to cool and solidify beneath the surface. If it does appear that an eruption is likely, the next problem involves deciding when it will start and what form it will take. Most importantly, a judgement has to be made on the likely scale of the forthcoming eruption, and when — during an ongoing eruptive sequence — the climactic event is likely to occur.

All these questions need to be answered in order that contingency plans involving evacuation and other measures can be activated at the appropriate time. This is now accomplished through establishing a scale of alert levels for which standard responses (eg, evacuation of successively more at-risk areas) are agreed in advance with the civil authorities. Even so, disagreements and misunderstandings do arise, often leading to major problems for the affected populations. On the Caribbean island of Guadeloupe in 1976, for example, over 70,000 people were needlessly evacuated for four months due to volcanologists misinterpreting the signs of unrest at the volcano. In sharp contrast, the aforementioned deaths at

BELOW LEFT: Methods for controlling the advance of lava flows.

BELOW: Remedial measures against the threat from lahars (mudflows).

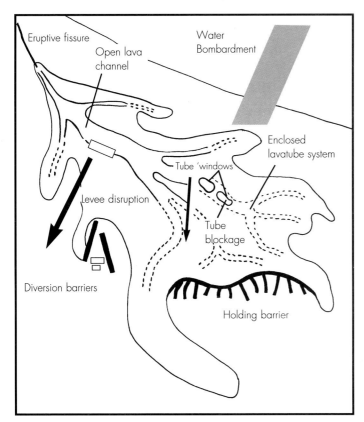

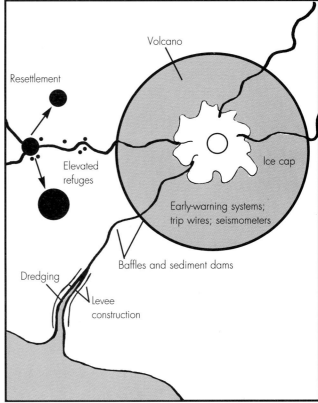

Nevado del Ruiz, resulted from the failure of the civil authorities to evacuate the threatened population even when told of the dangers by the scientists.

THE FUTURE

Around 50 volcanoes erupt every year, some of which — like the Mediterranean island of Stromboli — are constantly active, while others, such as Etna and Vesuvius in Italy or Krafla and Hekla in Iceland, may not have erupted for years or decades. As the length of this quiescent period is often proportional to the violence of the next eruption, of most concern are volcanoes which have not erupted for a century or more. These include Mounts Baker, Hood, Shasta, and Rainier in the western US, along with hundreds of dormant volcanoes in Southeast Asia, Central and South America, and around Pacific Rim. Problematically, because of our limited knowledge of the reactivation behaviour of such volcanoes, their future eruptions are also the most difficult to forecast.

It is very likely that the next really big eruption will occur at a volcano which has demonstrated no activity during historic times: in fact a dozen of the 16 largest explosive eruptions of the past two centuries occurred at volcanoes with no historical record of activity. Somewhat ominously, we have yet to experience a really BIG volcanic eruption — what is referred to by volcanologists as a VEI 8 event. These gigantic explosive eruptions typically eject thousands of cubic kilometres of debris into the atmosphere, devastating the surrounding region and dramatically modifying the global climate. Yellowstone caldera was excavated during a VEI 8 eruption around two million years ago, while a similar scale eruption at Toba (Indonesia) 74,000 years ago may have triggered the last ice age. Analysis of the frequencies of such huge eruptions suggests that they occur, on average, twice every one hundred thousand years, so there should be another along any time now.

BELOW RIGHT: Pinatubo's 1991 eruption ejected almost 10cu km (2.4cu miles) of magma. This amount is small compared with previous eruptions, such as those from Tambora (1815) and Toba (74,000 years ago). The illustration shows the areas which could have been buried beneath a kilometre (0.6 of a mile) of ash by these eruptions. In this case, Toba's products would have annihilated Greater London.

FAR RIGHT: A chain of lava fountains from the August 1971 fissure eruption of Kilauea in Hawaii. The fountains reach heights of hundreds of metres. The yellow interiors of the fountains, at about 1,100°C (2,012°F), are as much as 500°C (932°F) hotter than the deep-red outer layers.

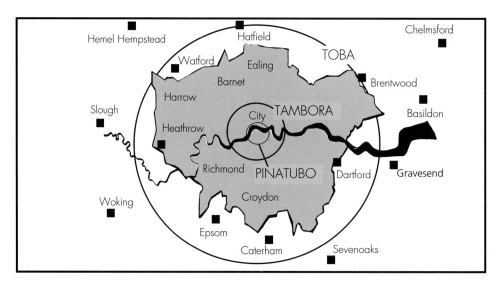

EUROPE

The end of Pompeii. An eyewitness account of Vesuvius erupting in August 79 AD, watched by Pliny the Younger from Capo Miseno, 30km (20 miles) distant.

There had been for several days some shocks from earthquakes, which hardly alarmed us because they are frequent in Campania; but that night they became so violent that one might think that the world was not being merely shaken, but turned upside-down ... Outside the houses we found ourselves in the midst of a strange and terrible scene. The coaches we had ordered out, though upon level ground, were sliding to and fro, and could not be kept steady ... Then we saw the sea sucked back and, as it were, repulsed by the convulsive motion of the earth ... and now many sea animals were captive on dry land ... On the other side, a black and dreadful cloud bursting out in gusts of igneous serpentine vapour now and again yawned open to reveal long, fantastic flames, resembling flashes of lightning but much larger. Soon afterwards the cloud I have described began to

Thirty-five centuries ago a tiny island in the Aegean burst into eruption, erasing an entire culture and inspiring one of the most enduring legends in the West. Releasing the energy of 3,000 atom bombs, a column of grey-black ash climbed towards the stratosphere while, 30km (20 miles) below, the sea was churned into a rabid cauldron by incandescent rock and gas. Tsunami washed along adjacent islands, including the shores of Minoan Crete, 120km (75 miles) south. Within hours, more than 65 billion tonnes of material had been redistributed across the Eastern Mediterranean — a dozen tonnes or so for every man, woman and child living today.

EIFEL VOLCANIC FIELD

CHAINE DES PUYS

ALBAN HILLS

OLOT VOLCANIC FIELD

VESUVIUS, CAMPI FLEGREI AND ISCHIA

AEOLIAN IS. (VULCANO, STROMBOLI)

ETNA

SANTORINI

The Bronze Age eruption was from Santorini (or Thera), at the time a key centre on the lucrative trade routes between Europe and North Africa. Hastening the decline of the Minoan civilization, the eruption has also been linked to the story of Atlantis, to heroic tales described for Jason and the Argonauts, and to the biblical account of Moses fleeing the Egyptian army. Of all eruptions on record, this event has most taxed the imagination of the public and the fantasy of scholars.

Santorini today is a popular tourist destination. Its sea-filled caldera, 7km (4 miles) across, provides shelter for local fishing boats and for invading cruise liners, all of which daily pass the emerging Nea Kameni, an islet growing from piles of lava slowly accumulating within. The island itself lies almost half-way along an uneven east-west chain of volcanoes, produced by the continuing northward collision of Africa into Europe (the same collision which started the uprise of the Alps some 40 million years ago). To the east, the chain stretches through Turkey and Armenia, before reaching the border between Russia and Georgia, where it links rather uncertainly with a volcanic line running towards the Red Sea; a wall painting from 6200 BC in Catal Hayuk, Central

descend upon the earth and to cover the sea . . . My mother beseeched me to escape as best I might: a young man could do it; she, burdened by age and corpulency, would die easy if only she had not caused my death. I replied I would not be saved without her . . . I looked behind me. A gross darkness pressed upon our rear and came rolling over the land as a torrent . . . We had scarce sat down when darkness overspread us, not like that of a moonless or cloudy night, but of a room when it is shut up, and the lamp put out. You could hear the shrieks of women, the crying of children, the shouts of men . . . I might have boasted that amidst dangers so appalling, not a sigh or expression of fear escaped me, had not my support been founded on that miserable consolation that all mankind were involved in the same calamity.

VOLCANO LOG: EUROPE
Active volcanoes and volcanic fields

Germany	1
France	1
Italy	13
Greece	5
Turkey	13
Russia (SW)	1
Georgia	4
Armenia	3
Total	41

The biggest and deadliest

VOLCANO	ERUPTION	VOL (cu km) ERUPTED	CASUALTIES
Santorini, Greece	1650 BC	30	Probably
Vesuvius, Italy	79 AD	2	3,500+ **PM**
	1631	0.3	4,000+ **PM**
	1906	0.3	350 **A**
	1944	0.1	27 **A**
Etna, Italy	1614–24	1	None
	1669	1	Some
	1843	0.05	56 **L**
Campi Flegrei, Italy	1538	0.03	24 **A**

Key: **A**=ash fall and/or falling blocks **D**=disease **F**=famine **G**=gases
L=landslides **La**=lavas **M**=mudflows **P**=pyroclastic flows **T**=tsunami

EUROPE

Personal Experiences

An anonymous eyewitness account of lava flows overrunning San Sebastiano on Vesuvius in March 1944.

Since the small hours of this morning lava from Vesuvius has been slowly eating its way through the village . . . In the darkness of the night, flames, the incandescent glow from the rolling masses of lava, and above all the great lambant tongue on the mountainside overhanging all, make it indescribably awesome, but daylight deprives it of much of its terror, and the flaming monster becomes just a gradually glowing coketip . . . The progress of destruction is almost maddeningly slow. There is nothing about it like the sudden wrath of devastation by bombing . . . As it gradually filled up the backyards of houses on the village street the flow seemed to pause. Very slowly the glowing mass piled itself up against the walls with all its weight. For a while it seemed as if it would engulf the houses as they stood but then, as the weight grew, a crack would appear in the wall. As it slowly widened first one wall would fall out and then the whole house would collapse and the mass would gradually creep over it, swallowing up the debris with it.

Turkey, provides the earliest known record of an eruption. To the west, the chain stretches across the Massif Central in Southern France (especially active 6,000-10,000 years ago) to just beyond the Spanish border, where the Olot volcanic field sits about 80km (50 miles) from Barcelona. Offset to the north, a cluster of volcanoes resides in the rifted Eifel district of Western Germany (for more on rifting see the next chapter, Africa and the Middle East), 60km (40 miles) from Luxembourg; although generally considered to have last erupted about 10,000 years ago, a recent examination of historical records hints that a minor eruption might actually have occurred in Gleichberg nearby as recently as 1783.

For the last 2,000 years, however, by far the most active region of the chain has been the southwest of Italy, from Naples through the Aeolian Islands and on south to Eastern Sicily. With the rise of the Roman Empire and the shift of power from the Aegean to the Western Mediterranean, eruptions from the Italian volcanoes became widely known across the ancient world, and most have been cited at one time or another as either the forge of Vulcan (the Roman god of war, from whose name volcano is derived) or the entrance to Hades. Seventeen hundred years later, the same volcanoes provided the spur for systematic observations of eruptions and these, in turn, laid the foundations for modern volcanology.

Best known of all is Vesuvius, the coastal sentinel that guards the southern approaches to Naples. Born just 25,000 years ago, the present Vesuvius edifice (or, more correctly, the Somma-Vesuvius edifice) is now 1,200m (4,000ft) tall. Its activity has been a heady cocktail of stately lava effusions and modest explosions, stirred by paroxysmal outbursts every few thousand years. The most recent paroxysm, in 79 AD, spewed forth more than 2cu km (70,000cu ft) of magma in less than four days (see Personal Experiences on pages 26 and 27). Just a few kilometres from the summit vent, the flourishing towns of Pompeii and Herculaneum were buried from sight (Pompeii by falling tephra, Herculaneum by pyroclastic flows) — to be rediscovered by accident 1,700 years later. Ironically, the eruption had started on 24 August, the day following what had once been the pagan festival to Vulcan.

Following the Pompeii disaster, Vesuvius erupted only occasionally until 1631, when it entered a period of activity that was to last almost continuously for 313 years. Most of the activity was effusive and contained within the summit crater, so that the volcano soom became an attraction for well-to-do travellers performing the Grand Tour from one European capital to the next. It was also during this period that Sir William Hamilton (British plenipotentiary to the court of Naples and long-suffering husband of Emma, more usually associated with Nelson) initiated systematic records of the

RIGHT: Snow at the summit of Mt Vesuvius, Europe's most famous volcano. The cone on the left, about 300m (1,000ft) high, has been built by a succession of eruptions between 1631 and 1944. The cone stands inside the flat-topped caldera of Mt Somma, formed by a series of catastrophic eruptions and collapses between 17,000 and 4,000 years ago. The 19th century lava flows in the foreground are today quarried for building stone.

CENTER RIGHT: Most of Etna's historical eruptions have produced lava flows. During vigorous effusions, such as the 1983 eruption, major lava streams can extend downslope by more than 10km (6 miles) to threaten nearby towns.

BELOW RIGHT: Other flows emerge more slowly to produce piles of lava streams only metres across and less than a kilometre (0.6 mile) long.

EUROPE

volcano's behaviour, followed 50 years later by the founding in 1845 of the world's first volcanological observatory.

Yet, just as major advances were being made in monitoring volcanoes, Vesuvius fell into repose. No eruptions have occurred since March 1944, the longest interval without activity since 1631. The tranquillity, on the one hand, has allowed full use to be made of the volcano's fertile and scenic slopes, now the home to more than 600,000 people; on the other hand, it is ominous for there is the worry that new magma is collecting a few kilometres beneath the volcano and, like a heating pressure cooker, is preparing to unleash another paroxysmal event.

Fear of an eruption is ever-present also on the western side of Naples, which overlooks the Campi Flegrei, a caldera 12km (7 miles) wide, open southwards to the Mediterranean, and less than 40,000 years old. In the last 10,000 years, some 15 eruptions have occurred across the floor of the caldera, most recently in 1538. Parts of the caldera have also been slowly rising and falling during at least historical times, especially along the coastline, from Pozzuoli (the St Tropez, or perhaps Malibu, of the Roman Empire) westwards to Capo Miseno (from where Pliny the Younger watched the AD 79

The build-up of explosive activity at the Northeast Crater on Mt. Etna in 1986.

RIGHT: The opening phase shows small clouds of dark ash pushing through more abundant clouds of white steam.

OVERLEAF, LEFT: After a few hours, the vent has cleared itself of old material, and the eruption feeds thick clouds that fill the crater and spill out over its sides (note the man in the foreground).

OVERLEAF, RIGHT: Twenty minutes later, the ash clouds are rising more forcefully just before lava fountains appeared several hundreds of metres high.

EUROPE

Vesuvius eruption, 30km (20 miles) away (see Personal Experience pages 24–25). Since 1970, in particular, Pozzuoli seems to have been riding a giant crustal blister that has pushed the town some 3.5m (11ft 6in) out of the sea. The simplest, and most alarming, explanation is that magma is slowly squeezing itself to the surface — alarming because 200,000 people live in Campi Flegrei, and because the last two pulses of uplift occurred only a decade apart in the 1970s and 1980s, fuelling speculation about what might happen before the turn of the century.

North from Campi Flegrei, the vestiges of volcanism are found from Roccamonfina, 60km (40 miles) from Vesuvius, to the geothermal fields of Lardarello in Tuscany, passing the hills around Rome, where activity may have occurred just over 2,000 years ago. South from Campi Flegrei, beyond its island volcanoes, Ischia and Procida (but not neighbouring Capri, which consists merely of limestone), it is but a day's journey by ferry to the seven Aeolian Islands, huddled together about 30km (20 miles) north of Sicily. Three of the islands are volcanically active: Lipari, which last erupted in 729 AD; Vulcano, last active in 1888; and Stromboli, the 'lighthouse of the Mediterranean', from whose summit the glow of magma has been visible for at least 2,000 years.

If Stromboli is the lighthouse, then Mt. Etna, 120km (75 miles) south, is the monarch. Rising 3,300m (11,000ft) above the seaboard of eastern Sicily, Etna's 500cu km (18 million cu ft) make it the largest continental volcano in Europe. At least half a million years old, the volcano's activity for the past 400 years has been dominated by effusive eruptions and so Etna has proved a natural laboratory for trying methods to change artificially the course of a lava flow (most recently in 1983 and 1992).

The first diversion attempts — the earliest of their kind known anywhere on record — were carried out on lavas from the 1669 eruption. Six weeks after the eruption had started on 11 March (from a low-lying vent 700m/2,300ft above sea level), lava flows reached the outer walls of Catania, a coastal town about 15km (10 miles) away. Wearing water-soaked skins to shield them from the lava's heat, Don Diego Pappalardo and 50 others used picks and axes to breach a hole in the cooled lava margin, close to the vent. As the lava flowed through the breach, a second band arrived from neighbouring Paternò, armed this time with weapons rather than tools. Fearing that the diverted lava would threaten Paternò, the second group encouraged the first one to disband. As a result, the breach healed itself, the flow resumed its original course, and much of Catania was destroyed, leaving 85% of its 20,000 inhabitants without a home. Such is the resilience of human nature, however, that Catania today has a population of over 400,000, is a major com-

ABOVE RIGHT: The Roman marketplace, Serapis, near the waterfront at Pozzuoli in Campi Flegrei. The area has risen and fallen several metres during the last 2,000 years. The dark bands on the three columns show an ancient sea level when the ground was depressed. The markings were caused by shellfish, living near the sea surface, boring holes into the columns.

BELOW RIGHT: Recent excavations around Vesuvius have exposed a new villa, the Villa dei Papiri, at the margins of the Roman town, Herculaneum. It was probably owned by Calpurnius Piso, who was related to the wife of Julius Caesar. Herculaneum was buried in AD 79 by a series of pyroclastic surges and flows. The total thickness of the deposits measures tens of metres. The summit of Vesuvius is just visible in the background.

EUROPE

BELOW RIGHT: Stromboli, one of the volcanic Aeolian Islands, has been in persistent eruption since at least Roman times.

BELOW: Rising above the outskirts of Naples, Vesuvius is surrounded by one of the most densely-populated regions on Earth. Even a small eruption would cause considerable damage.

FAR RIGHT: In September 1979, a small steam explosion from the summit of Etna showered some 200 tourists with giant boulders. Nine people were killed and over 20 seriously injured. Although the volcano was being monitored at the time, no warning signals were detected.

mercial port and, after the provincial capital Palermo, is the second city of Sicily.

The rapid return to normality shows the pull on human affairs of the fertility of volcanic soils. Twenty percent of Sicily's population live on the slopes of Etna which, because of its altitude, are among the island's major producers of citrus fruits and nuts. Throughout Italy, indeed, from Sicily to Lazio (not forgetting the ancient volcano Vulture, in Basilicata on Italy's east coast) soils fertilized by volcanoes have been a mainstay of the wine industry, including famous names such as Orvieto, Frascati and Lacryma Christi del Vesuvio. The next Italian wine in your glass might be the offspring of an eruption, so a toast to volcanoes would not be misplaced. *Salute!*

EUROPE

RIGHT: La Fossa crater on Vulcano, last active in 1888. Considered by the Romans to be the forge of the god Vulcan, the island has since given its name to all volcanoes.

CENTER RIGHT: Nea Kameni, the active volcanic island growing from the submerged caldera of Santorini, whose cataclysmic eruption about 1650 BC has often been linked to the fall of Atlantis. Nea Kameni is slowly growing by the accumulation of lavas, its last eruption occurring in 1950.

BELOW RIGHT: Part of the wall of the Santorini caldera formed about 1650 BC. Today it is a major tourist attraction and port-of-call for cruise ships and island ferries.

FAR RIGHT: Etna's summit is dominated by two pits, the Chasm and Bocca Nuova, whose adjoining wall, weakened by volcanic gases, is slowly collapsing. When the two pits merge, the region will consist of a giant depression hundreds of metres across and more than 100m (328ft) deep.

EUROPE

RIGHT: Lava flows from Etna's 1991–93 eruption destroyed orchards on the outskirts of Zafferana, one of the main towns on the volcano's eastern flank. Several attempts were made to divert the lava, which ultimately halted outside the town.

CENTER RIGHT: The Bocca Nuova pit, over100m (328ft) across and deep, at the summit of Mt Etna. It was from this vent that a steam explosion killed nine people in 1979. (See caption for photograph on page 35.)

BELOW RIGHT: Etna's coastal flank is cut by the Valle del Bove (Valley of the Oxen), an amphitheatre 4km (2.5 miles) across and 1km (0.6 mile) deep. For the last few thousand years, the valley has been gradually filled by lava flows, seen as the dark streams in the foreground. Behind the valley, small steam clouds can be seen above Etna's summit complex.

FAR RIGHT: Sulphurous steam rises persistently from the floor of La Solfatara, one of several cones found across the floor of the Campi Flegrei caldera, west of Naples. Some visitors consider the fumes to have medicinal properties; most maintain a respectful distance.

AFRICA AND THE
MIDDLE EAST

When the forebears of the human race first stood upon two legs, they were almost certainly within sight of an active volcano. Fossil remains at Olduvai Gorge, in Tanzania, show that two million years ago early hominids and other wild animals roamed the plains of Ngorogoro, a giant volcanic caldera 700m (2,300ft) deep and 22km (14 miles) across while, 200km (125 miles) away, the young Kilimanjaro (Shining Mountain) was still several eruptions short of becoming the highest mountain in Africa.

Of all places on Earth, man had chosen to evolve where a continent was intent on breaking apart. The scars from the attempt remain today as the Geat Rift Valley, a depression some 100km (600 miles) wide that runs north from Beira (Mozambique) to the Valley

VOLCANO LOG: AFRICA AND THE MIDDLE EAST

Numbers of active volcanoes and volcanic fields

AFRICA

Ethiopia	66
Djibouti	4
Red Sea	2
Kenya	21
Tanzania	10
Uganda	7
Zaire	4
Rwanda	3
Nigeria	1
Cameroon	4
Bioko	3
Libya	1
Chad	4
Sudan	5

MIDDLE EAST

Syria	6
Saudi Arabia	8
Yemen	6
South Yemen	3
Gulf of Aden	1
Oman	1
Iran	5
Afghanistan	2
Total	167

Ol Doinyo Lengai has been almost continuously erupting since 1983. The activity of this remarkable volcano is described by Jacques Durieux on pages 52–53.

The biggest and deadliest

VOLCANO	ERUPTION	VOL (cu km) ERUPTED	CASUALTIES
Dubbi, Ethiopia	1861	0.03?	106?
Nyamuragira, Zaire	1912	0.04?	20 L
	1938	0.2?	—
Nyiragongo, Zaire	1977	0.02?	70 L
Monoun, Cameroon	1984	N/A	37 G
Nyos, Cameroon	1986	N/A	1,700+ G
Harat Rahat, Saudi Arabia	1256	0.2?	—

Key: **A**=ash fall and/or falling blocks **D**=disease **F**=famine **G**=gases
L=landslides **La**=lavas **M**=mudflows **P**=pyroclastic flows **T**=tsunami

of Jordan; 6,500km (4,000 miles) long (almost 20 times the length of the Grand Canyon), the rift has gouged a path across one-sixth of the globe's circumference and contains some of the most spectacular but least-known volcanoes on the planet.

Hardly 150 years have passed since Western missionaries and explorers first penetrated the African interior. Until that time, only a handful of eruptions had been reported, and these mostly from coastal volcanoes, so that all notion of volcanic activity rested with tribal legends and tales of distant 'fireplains', into which even the bravest of native hunters feared to adventure. Since then, more than 110 eruptions have been recorded from 18 locations, while another 112 volcanoes have been diagnosed as potentially active.

About 80 percent of the volcanoes are found alongside or within the Great Rift Valley. The most southerly are dominated by three massifs, of which the greatest is Kilimanjaro, 6,000cu km (8 million cu yd) of lavas and pyroclastics that tower to 5,967m (19,572ft) above sea level (and more than 5km/3 miles above the surrounding grasslands), where summit snows form an incongruous backdrop to life on the Equator. In comparison, neighbouring Mt Meru (the Black Mountain) appears but a modest companion, rising to an elevation of just 4,568m (14,983m). However, 75km (45 miles) from Kilimanjaro, the Black Mountain is not complete. Its summit has been worn down by ancient glaciers, while massive collapses have removed 3km (2 miles) of its eastern flank (compare Santa Maria in Guatemala, in the chapter on Mexico and Central America).

Unlike Meru and Kilimanjaro, Ol Doinyo Lengai, the Mountain of God and last of the trio, lies on the floor of the rift valley. With a summit at 2,880m (9,446ft), the rose-grey flanks of the volcano blend imperceptibly into the shores of Lake Natron, itself bathed a red-pink by resident flamingoes. It is by far the most active of the southern triumvirate, boasting some 15 eruptions in 100 years, compared with three for Meru and only fumarolic emissions from Kilimanjaro. The activity, though, is unusual, for the modern products are rich in carbon dioxide and have a chemistry closely similar to that of washing soda (sodium carbonate). In legend as well, Ol Doinyo Lengai stands apart from other volcanoes because it is seen not as a menace, but as a great provider, the thunder of its eruptions being the noise of cattle about to emerge from the crater. (As with many native traditions, the legend remains even more curious than reality: which would keep you more alert — stampeding cattle or packets of soap powder?)

North of Ol Doinyo Lengai, the rift valley dissects Kenya with another 16 active centres, from Longonot, Suswa and Menengai to Teleki-Likaiyu and volcanic islands in the middle of Lake Rudolf. Like Meru and Kilimanjaro, several of the centres support summit

RIGHT: Chaimu, part of the Chyulu Hills volcanic complex in Kenya's Tsavo National Park. The complex consists of a collection of craters and cones, most recently active in the 1850s.

calderas, excellent examples of how the tops of mature volcanoes can easily founder. Since 1870, less than a dozen eruptions have been reported, mostly small effusions of lava from Teleki-Likaiyu and the impressively-named Emuruangogolak. There is little doubt, however, that bigger eruptions lie in store for the millennium to come.

Eruptions have been much more frequent 700km (400 miles) further west, beyond Lake Victoria and within a second branch of the Great Rift Valley. At the junction of Zaire, Rwanda and Uganda stand the Virunga volcanoes, the cause of 80 percent of African volcanism since colonization began. The last home of the Great Apes, the volcanoes rise above 3,000m (9,840ft), their peaks often lost behind low-lying cloud. Activity is focused upon the neighbours Nyiragongo and Nyamuragira, enormous volcanoes built by lavas that are surprisingly fluid, topped by calderas over a kilometre across and perpetually filled by lakes of glowing lava.

From the 1930s until 1977, the most famous of all lava lakes was that within Nyiragongo. For more than four decades, the midnight glow from the lake lured climbers and geologists from the four corners of the globe. Then at 10.15 on the morning of 10 January 1977, a fissure from beneath the summit cut the south side of the volcano, allowing the sudden drainage of the lake onto slopes 10km (6 miles) away. The lava swept downslope more than 5km (3 miles), burning villages in its wake and, by 10.35, 70 people lay dead, their life roasted away in a peculiarly horrible fashion. Today all that is left is a veneer of black lava, a metre thick at its front, but only millimetres deep close to the fissure.

The unexpected outpouring from Nyiragongo produced the greatest known number of victims from a lava flow. The tragedy of that day lives on in the memory of the volcano's inhabitants, including the 200,000 population of Goma. Not only did the 1977 flow reach within 3km (2 miles) from Goma airport but, after the caldera's rapid drainage, its unstable walls collapsed inwards, vaporizing trapped water and sending clouds of muddy steam into the city. Since 1982, the caldera has again filled with lava, resurrecting the spectre of another disaster, an anxiety not helped in the mid-1990s by the arrival near Goma of 750,000 war refugees from Rwanda.

Persistent lava lakes are one of the hallmarks of Africa's historic volcanism. Another renowned example is the lake at Erta Ale, 2,000km (1,200 miles) from Virunga. Erta Ale (the Fuming, or Devil's, Mountain) lies near the northeast end of the Rift Valley segment that runs across Ethiopia and Djibouti, from Lake Rudolf to the Red Sea. In the 1930s the volcano was felt to be a spent force — a view upset 30 years later by the growth of a lava lake that remains active today.

ABOVE RIGHT: The summit crater of Ol Doinyo Lengai in Tanzania. Fresh dark lava can be seen in the foreground. The products from this volcano are unusually rich in carbon dioxide, often resembling the composition of washing soda.

BELOW RIGHT:
Mt. Cameroon, Cameroon, is the largest volcanic edifice in West Africa. It last erupted in 1982, during filming of Greystoke, when lava flows destroyed farmland and threatened rubber plantations.

The summit lava lake at Erta Ale sits at an elevation of about 500m (1,600ft), while the base of the volcano rests 75m (250ft) below sea level. Born within the Danakil depression, Erta Ale and its neighbours have grown from the most low-lying part of the Great Rift Valley on land. One hundred kilometres away, the rift has been flooded to create the Red Sea, whose floor is identical to that beneath the world's oceans. After rifting had started 20 million years ago, the crust of the continent eventually split between modern Ethiopia and Arabia, allowing a new crust to form from upwelling lava. Indeed, what is happening now at the Red Sea is possibly what happened between the American and Afro-European continents when the Atlantic first developed 200 million years ago.

Whether or not the Red Sea will evolve into a wide ocean is uncertain. To widen further, it must push Africa southwest. However, Africa is already being pushed northeastwards by the Atlantic, and which ocean will win remains to be seen. Meanwhile, the competition has ensured sporadic volcanism also along the Red Sea's Arabian coastline and beyond, to as far north as Damascus in Syria and, eastwards, into Iran and Afghanistan. Although only a few historic eruptions have been recorded (from 500 AD to, most recently, the small 1937 eruption near Dhamar in Yemen), accounts from the Old Testament (try *Isaiah* 34: 9–10) suggest that volcanism has played a significant role in the cultural development of the region.

Rifting has also been essential to Africa's second great chain of volcanoes, which runs for 1,600km (1,000 miles) along the Cameroon-Nigeria border to the lonely island of Pagalu, in the Gulf of Guinea. The Y-shaped chain is dominated by Mt Cameroon (the Cavern of the Gods) which, rising from the coast to 4,070m (13,350ft), is the highest peak in West Africa. Due to an eruption in the 5th century BC, Mt. Cameroon became the first volcano outside the Mediterranean known to the west's ancient world. Its last eruption in 1982 coincided with location filming for Greystoke, providing a spectacle even more dramatic than that of Tarzan. Curiously, the volcanic chain lies not inside, but alongside a Y-shaped rift, the Benue Trough, in Nigeria. It seems that the rifting 65 million years ago jolted the crust sufficiently to shift the line of ascending magma 250km (800 miles) southeast, a clear demonstration of the power that drives plate tectonics.

Two hundred kilometres (125 miles) inland, many of the volcanoes have water lakes filling their summit craters. Twice in the 1980s (at Lake Monoun in 1984 and Lake Nyos in 1986), clouds of carbon dioxide unexpectedly escaped from the lake waters and, being heavier than air, they rolled downslope close to the ground, before dissipating into the atmosphere. Together, the silent, deadly

ABOVE: The carbonatitic volcano Kerimasi, twin to Ol Doinyo Lengai in Tanzania.

LEFT: Masai farmers tend their cattle in the shadow of Meru, the Black Mountain.

clouds suffocated more than 1,700 people and hundreds of cattle and wild animals. Though the volcanoes were not obviously active, it appears that carbon dioxide may have been seeping gently and undetected into the base of the lakes. Once enough gas had been dissolved, the waters in the lakes became critically stable, so that only a small disturbance (perhaps heavy rainfall, or a weak earth tremor) could force the lake water to overturn, bringing the gas-rich layers to the surface and allowing the carbon dioxide to bubble out and escape. Several ways of reducing the hazard are currently being studied, and include siphoning away the gases before they achieve dangerous concentrations. Whatever the methods finally chosen, the lakes of Cameroon show that not even a sleeping volcano can be ignored.

ABOVE RIGHT: Summit activity at Ol Doinyo Lengai is contained within a small collapsed caldera.

BELOW RIGHT: In addition to lava flows, the carbonatite magmas can produce small conical hornitoes as (FAR RIGHT) lava bubbles up through the vent.

RIGHT: An expedition makes a desert halt between Ol Doinyo Lengai and Lake Natron, renowned for its flamingo population.

BELOW: Volcanic crater lake on the 'craters' trail' in Uganda's Rwenzori National Park. Water-filled crater lakes are common in Africa, especially along the Cameroon line, from which sudden releases of carbon dioxide killed villagers around Lakes Monoun and Nyos in the 1980s.

FAR RIGHT: Ol Doinyo Lengai was considered beneficial by local tribes, who believed that eruptions heralded the arrival of wild animals for hunting and farming.

Ol Doinyo Lengai

Ol Doinyo Lengai, situated 200km to the west of Kilamanjaro, is one of numerous volcanoes scattered over the bottom of the East African rift valley.

Lengai has two special characteristics: it is the only constantly active volcano in the east of the Rift, and the composition of its lava flows make it of unique geological importance. The magma comes out of the African mantle, through ample beds of limestone and is the source of extraordinary silica-deficient but calcium and sodium-rich lava. Indeed, on the surface the lava one finds is so strange it almost needs another name; possessing no silica it seems rather to be a kind of molten limestone, unstable and in fusion: carbonatite. This strange material was only discovered in the 1960s because Lengai is so difficult to reach and its ascent so arduous, that despite its scientific interest, research expeditions are extremely rare. I remember my 1992 expedition:

No porters in the area; since we left Arusha, our landrover has had to carry all the kit and the porters who will carry it up to the crater.

In our base camp, at the foot of the volcano, the last rucksacks are buckled up at nightfall: everything must be ready for a rapid departure at three o'clock the next morning.

At the appointed time, our headlamps light up high grasses, but these soon disappear, giving place to steep cinder slopes that make ascent difficult as we slide back with each step forward. Higher still, the volcano protects itself even more successfully with huge slabs of virtually smooth rock defending the summit.

In constant fear of falling, on foot and on all fours, the team slowly makes its way towards what seems to be the summit. We feel as if we're walking in the sky, an impression reinforced when the sun rises from below the crater rim. Then, abruptly,we drop onto a lunar landscape.

In front of us is a vast circular crater, colourless, white and grey, with strange chimneys in the centre almost caricatures with their straight sides and the little trails of vapor crowning them. All around is a horizontal platform whose surface is scarred with old lava flows superipmosed one over the other. Silence reigns dense and thick in this other world: we really have fallen on the moon . . .

After the first few minutes of awestruck contemplation, we fling ourselves to the centre of the crater — is the volcano active at the moment? Where is this carbonatite that we have dreamed about so much? Are there lava flows?

Our steps crack a kind of crystalline crust that covers the surface of the crater: carbonatite decomposed by atmospheric agents . . . But where is the fresh lava? The mineral world that surrounds us is entirely

Silhouetted against the skyline, one of our party looks into the crater.

frozen. Without stopping, and a little disappointed, we turn back — the volcano is extinct!

Soon a large and imposing cone draws our attention, caparisoned with white lava-flows, it dominates the crater with its strange shape. Two black holes on its summit tell us of the existence of chimneys inside the cone.

Who could resist the curiosity? Leaning over the first one a violent blast of heat drives us back immediately — there's the coveted carbonatite!

About ten metres beneath our feet, at the bottom of a bell-shaped well, a lake of lava boils cheerfully away. Its appearance is astonishing, a kind of chestnut-coloured mix topped with an imposing scum: the volcanic gasses here have made a strange foamy bath! From time to time, the emissions of gas diminish in intensity, the foam subsides, and the lake is covered with an elastic skin which slowly swells and ebbs.

If this spectacle fascinates us, it also asks us a crucial question — how are we going to sample the bottom of this well? We find the answer at the bottom of the second chimney. It also contains a lake of lava, but much smaller than that of its neighbour. One of the sides of this chimney is notched by a narrow canyon which we succeeded in scaling, and which allows us access to an outcrop a few metres from the surface of the lake: from there we can reach it.

The following morning found us again at the edge of the well. Ropes and harnesses in place, gas-mask on, I let myself slide slowly into the crevice which leads to the lava-lake. The heat is bearable, but the volcanic gases are very highly concentrated in carbon dioxide, which the mask does not filter very effectively — it is necessary to work very quickly. In front of me, the crust covering the lake is pierced by two chimneys, overflowing with scum and with lava in fusion: it's the ideal spot from which to take our samples! Many researchers are interested in this unique rock, and today we have the chance to provide samples from the base of the chimney that climbs through the crust from the bowels of the earth. Samples of gas next, and we succeed in filling up some phials with the high temperature gas.

In the following days, we witness the lava-lake overflowing several times — a fascinating spectacle. The carbonatite flows, liquid as water and black as ink, hurl themselves down veritable canyons before pouring out onto the ground of the crater. Another strange sight is their change of colour when they contact air and during their cooling off: they rapidly change from black to chestnut and within a few hours from chestnut to white.

It's this white lava, carried in the form of fine cinders and dusts, which has marked so much the proud Masai who traverse the plains at the foot of the volcano. Ol Doinyo Lengai, in their language, means 'God's Place'.

ABOVE: Conical hornito in the crater.

LEFT: Jacques Durieux takes samples.

ABOVE RIGHT: Masai warriors on the veldt before 'God's Place'.

RIGHT: Cinder slopes made ascent difficult.

Erta Ale

Slowly the steel cable unrolls into the throat of the teflon guide. I find the sensation both familiar and surprising — like being seated in a climbing harness. In fact, I feel rigged up like an astronaut in my huge canvas suit, with rucksack full, climbing equipment swinging about from my belt, fat leather gloves, protective eye goggles, gas-mask in hand, climbing boots, and a two-way radio with which to keep in contact with my companions.

Having descended but a few metres, I find myself in empty space, hanging at the end of a cable that suddenly seems very fragile. Forcing myself to control the irresistable rotation, I try to aid my descent by placing my feet on the wall of rock which faces me. The wall is rather unstable, one only has to brush against it to detach large lumps that fall with enormous crashes. The atmosphere is harsh and conditions relatively difficult.

At the moment of departure, stepping over the rim of the well into empty space, I couldn't help a little twinge of fear. But that is part of the thrill of adventure. While I spin on the end of my cable my view sweeps across the crater; 80m (260ft) lower down, the lava-lake is stirred by fountains of lava and the skin that covers it in some cooler spots makes it seem alive and breathing.

Rather than fear or apprehension, I feel that I am in my element; at home in the middle of the crater wall — Erta'Ale is a volcano that I have dreamed about for years.

Metre by metre the rock wall unfolds in front of me, made up of lava flows piled precariously one on the other, seemingly ready to fall at any moment. But I have already known similar rockwalls and had learnt to overcome them. At last the bottom draws near. Under my feet an enormous pile of debris formed by previous collapses of the crater. It is completely covered in a thick bed of dust, fine cinders and needles of glass thrown up by the fountains that animate the lake of molten lava. Taking care the crust is easily negotiated, 30m (100ft) more of descent allow me to reach a platform of sorts formed by previous overflowings of the lava-lake. In spite of the warnings by radio from my companions above, I cannot resist the temptation to lean out over the lake.

Scarlet fountains, waves of gold and incandescent jets of molten lava greet me. A blast of super-hot air forces me to retreat quickly. Here I am again in a world of lights, sounds and smells, as if at the centre of the earth . . . Above my head the crater cuts a perfect circle of sky which begins to cloud; below me, a perfect circle of molten lava; exactly between the two — me, suspended.

It is the realization of a dream of a quarter of a century . . . and, thank goodness, it is good that the reality lives up to expectations!

Returning to base camp, our Ethiopian assistants recount various legends. For them Erta Ale is the mountain in which the devil dwells. When I told them I that I had met no one at the bottom of the crater, they replied with humour that there were only little timid devils there, but the big one, the real one, is there behind the crest of the caldera, and it would do no good to go and see him!

Getting to Erta Ale is far from easy — just to reach the

RIGHT: The Erta Ale crater.

volcano is a test of endurance. The volcano is situated at the bottom of the Danakil Depression, generally considered to be one of the most inhospitable regions on earth, a valley floor 120m below sea level. The climactic conditions are terrible, with record temperatures — 56°C (133°F) in the shade, but with no shade to be found there.

The following day saw much activity on the rim of the crater, with the endess work of winching exhausting those who had to brace themselves against the handles, and a leaden sun beating down making conditions unfavourable for this kind of work. But swiftly men and equipment are ferried back onto the platform which forms the steep banks of the lava-lake, at the foot of the debris mass. This platform overhangs the lake by some 10m (30ft). We are going to work there all day, and have to protect ourselves from the intense heat of the molten lava. The lava of Erta'Ale is basalt, which remains molten at a temperature of 1,100°C (2,012°F). The lake has a surface area of 4,000sq m (43,000sq ft), so the thermal radiation is intense. To lean over the side without protection is out of the question. Just to have a quick look we must position gloved hands in front of our faces, longer and something more serious must be used. Fortunately we have our suits of aluminiumised Nomex, which are fireproof and their shiny surface is designed to reflect back inra-red radiation. To protect the eyes, we use a sheet of polished gold; its only a few microns thick and so see-through.

Dressed in our armour, we can at last approach the edge and take some time to admire the view afforded us. The surface of the lake is covered in a layer of cooler lava, floating on the molten core like the skin on milk. The lake is moving — a current ripples the lava and makes the skin undulate. This current originates in a fountain spraying molten lava brewed by the high temperature gas that it emits. The skin is black in the shade, and as brilliant as silver in the sun; the fountain is scarlet, becoming orange as its temperature rises. The flow of the lava tears the skin into huge panels separated by fissures through which the lava shows red. Bubbles of gas regularly break the surface of the lake, popping the elastic skin with spurts and incandescent jets. This constant show continued throughout the day of sample-taking, the samples of lava and gas accumulating making this adventure a real scientific expedition. What more could an adventurous vulcanologist wish for?

Nyiragongo

We all dream of volcanoes on fire, with incandescent lava and majestic craters . . . but often nature forces us to be more humble. Today our dreams of volcanoes are set against wading in the mud of a damp track, in a soaking forest where the tree trunks hide murkily in the mist.

Another hour of climbing: my companions are giving me funny looks, asking where the hell I'm leading them. But the stiff slope interrupts brusquely and then a few sombre rocks stand out of the mist which is now being stirred by an icy wind. We are at the summit of the volcano.

At our feet is a cliff face of dangerous rock vanishing into the mist. Grumblings, or rather some kind of gigantic snorting, drifts up from below, making our teeth chatter. The disappointment of my companions almost turns to hostility but I manage to persuade them to descend the 200m (650ft) vertical rockface that guards the entrance to the crater. After two hours spent ferrying equipment and establishing a camp on the first platform, an unexpected break in the mist gives us the chance to penetrate the inside of the central well.

An enormous spur, as if broken off from the first platform, descends towards the centre of the crater. At the end of the spur we overhang a lake of molten lava, a few metres away from its surface. Calm at the moment, it is covered in an elastic skin which shines with a magnificent metallic glare in the sunlight. This skin undulates and inflates slowly above the pulsating lava. Suddenly, the whole lake bursts into life. At one end the lava suddenly spurts in a fountain which makes a rounded dome. Feeding the continuous flow of this fountain, the other end of the lake sinks rapidly into a glowing red cave. Activity starts again with fountains bursting into life all around the circumference of the lake at the foot of the rockface. Some of these gush out right up to the platform, and bigger and bigger bubbles of gas burst with huge detonations; the speed of the outflow accelerates . . . a new fountain of lava is born at our feet, some burning drops rain around us — we would like to watch longer, but the wall of heat drives us back.

We do not believe that vulcanology and asceticism should inevitably be synonymous, and our camps are often well provisioned. Today we have really done well and we are a bit bombed after a copious dinner and a celebratory drink. Collapsed in the tent, we were remodelling the world with the help of a bottle of rum when one of the team calls out that something is going on in the crater and that we should check it out! When we reach the edge of the fire well, it's like a festival . . . the lava-lake suddenly inflates and erupts into the whole depression. Almost 320,000sq m (3.5 million sq ft) of molten lava spreads out in front of us, with fountains spurting, waves of lava 5m (16ft) high and 100m (328ft) long sweep the whole crater. There is no scale to measure by, no words to describe the view. We experience a storm of sensations, of hot winds, of sounds and smells . . .

Later on that night the phenomenon subsides a little; we slowly cross the whole crater to rejoin our camp and see once again the star-studded sky cut off above the glowing red rockface that surrounds us. It's just an ordinary visit to the volcano Niyiragongo.

RIGHT: Niyiragongo lights up the night sky.

ABOVE: *Our camp on the edge of the crater.*

LEFT and RIGHT: *'. . . fountains bursting into life all around the circumference of the lake at the foot of the rockface. Some of these gush out right up to the platform, and bigger and bigger bubbles of gas burst with huge detonations; the speed of the outflow accelerates . . . a new fountain of lava is born at our feet, some burning drops rain around us — we would like to watch longer, but the wall of heat drives us back.'*

63

ASIA

There is very little that mere mortals can do when the gods of both the underworld and the sea, Vulcan and Neptune, combine forces to do their worst. This deadly alliance last appeared in 1883, when the slumbering volcanic island of Krakatoa awakened violently to wreak havoc across southern Sumatra and eastern Java, and to write its name large in the book of the greatest volcanic explosions of historical times.

As a small, uninhabited island in the Sunda Strait between Java and Sumatra, Krakatoa had attracted little attention from the populations of neighbouring islands, and it is likely that many in Batavia (now Jakarta) did not even know of its existence. All this changed, however, at the end of May, 1883, when loud explosions marked the

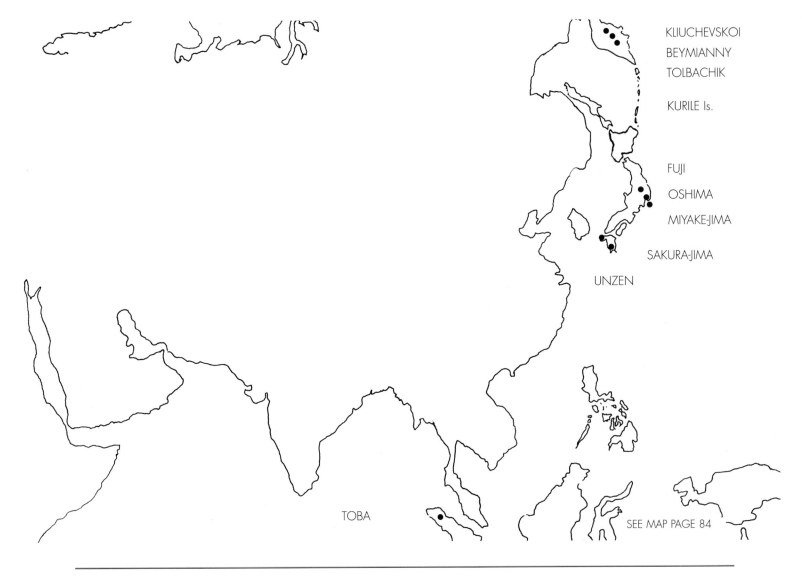

KLIUCHEVSKOI
BEYMIANNY
TOLBACHIK

KURILE Is.

FUJI
OSHIMA
MIYAKE-JIMA
SAKURA-JIMA
UNZEN

TOBA

SEE MAP PAGE 84

onset of a new eruption. Activity continued, alternating with peaceful interludes, throughout June and July, generating curiosity but little concern from the people of Batavia and neighbouring towns. From 1.00pm on 26 August, however, the volcano finally caught the complete attention of the local population, with a series of titanic explosions loud enough to be heard throughout Java, which hoisted a great black cloud over 25km (16 miles) above the island. The entry into the sea of pyroclastic flows generated the first of a series of tsunami waves which began to pound the shores of Java and Sumatra with increasing violence. Throughout the night of the 26th,

VOLCANO LOG: ASIA

Numbers of active volcanoes and volcanic fields

China	11
Indochina	11
Indonesia and Andaman Islands	141
Japan and neighbouring islands	113
Korea	4
Mongolia	5
Philippines	54
Russia	18
Total	528

The biggest and the deadliest

VOLCANO	ERUPTION	VOL (cu km) ERUPTED	CASUALTIES
Toba, Indonesia	72000BC	2,200	—
Kelut, Indonesia	1586	1	10,000 M?
Asama, Japan	1783	0.1	1,500 MP
Unzen, Japan	1792	0.1	15,000 LT
Tambora, Indonesia	1815	40	92,000 AF
Galunggung, Indonesia	1822	1	4,000 P
Shiveluch, Russia	1854	2	—
Awu, Indonesia	1856	0.1	2,800 M
Krakatau, Indonesia	1883	6	36,000 T
Bandai-san, Japan	1883	0.1	500 L
Taal, Philippines	1911	0.1	1,400 P
Kelut, Indonesia	1919	0.1	5,110 M
Merapi, Indonesia	1930	0.01	1,369 P
Bezymianny, Russia	1956	1	—
Agung, Indonesia	1963	0.1	1,184 PM
Tolbachik, Russia	1975	2	—
Unzen, Japan	1991	0.01	43 P
Pinatubo, Philippines	1991	7	800 PMD

Key: **A**=ash fall and/or falling blocks **D**=disease **F**=famine **G**=gases **L**=landslides **La**=lavas **M**=mudflows **P**=pyroclastic flows **T**=tsunami

Personal Experiences

Sir Stamford Raffles reports on the eruption of Tambora in 1815.

The eruption began on April 5th and did not quite cease until July. There were first detonations, which were heard in Sumatra, a distance of nearly 931 miles, and were taken for discharges of artillery. Three distinct columns of flame rose to an immense height, and the whole surface of the mountain soon appeared covered with incandescent lava, which extended to enormous distances; stones, some as large as the head, fell in a circle of several miles diameter, and the fragments dispersed in the air caused total darkness . . . The explosion lasted 34 days, and the abundance of the ashes expelled was such that at Java, a distance of 310 miles, they caused complete darkness in midday, and covered the ground and roofs with stratum several inches thick. At Sambawa also, the region near the volcano was entirely devastated, and the houses destroyed with 12,000 inhabitants. Thirty six persons only escaped the disaster. The trees and pasturages were buried deeply under pumice and ashes. At Bima, 40 miles from the volcano, the weight of the ashes was such that the roofs were crushed in. The floating pumice in the sea formed an island three feet in thickness, that the vessels could scarcely pass through.

Personal Experiences

Volcanology is a dangerous business, and 12 volcanologists have died 'in action' over the past six years. The 19th century French scientist, Daniel Lièvre describes graphically the terror of being caught in a volcanic explosion at the summit of the Japanese volcano, Kirishima.

I look at the crater. A thick column of white vapours, smoke, and grey ashes is rising into the sky, lit up by red lights that set it ablaze like lightning. At a glance I calculate the extreme point where this rain of projectiles is going to fall . . . it would require ten minutes, maybe more, to be out of danger and, in a few seconds, the ground will be covered with stones and scoria on fire. Fleeing is useless. Death is certain. I take out my watch. It is 8.35. In less than a minute it will all be over. I find myself in the middle of a sphere of fire . . . a piece of rock hits me on the head. I sprawl on the ground, face down . . . A shower of stones falls on to my back . . . Around me are falling incandescent blocks which make deep holes in the ground and cover me with their fragments . . . I find myself standing up, I don't know how. Since death has consented to spare me, I shall try to flee. I leave my hat smoking and start to descend.

people cowered in their homes which shook and rattled as if targeted by an artillery bombardment. All this time, pyroclastic flows continued to enter the sea while huge volumes of pumice were blasted high into the atmosphere, together evacuating a great void beneath the volcano, and setting the scene for one of the most catastrophic volcanic events on record.

The climax came at 10am on 27 August, when the roof of the partly emptied magma chamber — no longer able to support the weight of the volcano above — fractured and collapsed. Seawater and magma met and mixed within seconds to generate a cataclysmic explosion heard as far away as Australia and the Indian Ocean, hurling ash and pumice to a height of 50km (30 miles). Vulcan's work was by now largely done, but Neptune ensured that there was little respite, as towering tsunami over 40m (130ft) high swept out in all directions from what remained of the volcano, scouring the neighbouring coasts of Sumatra and Java, and taking the lives of 36,000 people in nearly 300 towns and villages. Such was the power of the waves that the Dutch warship *Berouw* was carried over a kilometre inshore, to be left high and dry 10m (30ft) above sea level. Throughout the climactic events, total darkness reigned, in some places for over two days, and hot ash fell at a rate of 15cm (4in) in 10 minutes at times, making both seeing and breathing almost impossible. These appalling conditions continued throughout the night of the 27th and the morning of the 28th until, later that day, the explosions finally ceased and the silence of the graveyard settled over the half-buried towns.

The death of Krakatoa reverberated, literally, around the world, and nine days later barometer needles still wavered as atmospheric shockwaves continued to circumnavigate the planet — four times in all. Tidal gauges far from Indonesia also recorded the enormous disturbances in the oceans caused by the collapse of the island, and some reports suggest that effects of the tsunami were even observed in the UK. Another legacy of Krakatoa's demise was the brilliant sunsets resulting from the huge quantities of fine ash ejected high into the atmosphere and dispersed across the planet by high-altitude winds. Rose-tinted twilights are reported from Europe and North America, which persisted for hours after sunset, while the phrase 'once in a blue moon' lost much of its meaning as variously coloured moons and suns made their appearance.

Asia teems with the most explosive and dangerous volcanoes, a legacy of the complex plate tectonics of the region which ensures a plethora of subduction zones within which large volumes of new magma are constantly being formed. There are over 500 active and potentially active volcanoes in all, most forming a

ABOVE: Merapi has been one of Java's most destructive volcanoes. Since 1900, more than 25 villages have been destroyed by pyroclastic flows, triggered by the collapse of the lava dome growing at its summit.

LEFT: Ashfall from Pinatubo's 1991 eruption met little resistance from makeshift dwellings around the volcano.

continuous string which heads south and east from Sumatra and through Java and Bali, before heading north into the Philippines and Japan. From here, the volcanic island chain of the Kuriles links Japan to the Kamchatka peninsula of eastern Russia; truly a land of fire and ice.

The region is home to three of the biggest volcanic bangs ever. In addition to the destruction of Krakatoa, two other Indonesian volcanoes have also exploded into life with sufficient violence as to dramatically affect the Earth's climate. During 1815 as Wellington and Napoleon fought for military dominance in Europe, the Tambora volcano on the island of Sumbawa, was preparing to unleash the greatest eruption since the retreat of the glaciers 10,000 years ago (see Personal Experience page 65). Following three years of rumblings, a series of tremendous explosions on 10 and 11 April turned day into night and dumped huge thicknesses of ash over Sunbawa itself and the neighbouring islands of Bali and Java.

As well as the 12,000 deaths resulting from the direct effects of the eruption, another 80,000 starved or succumbed to disease as crops died and water was contaminated. The effects were not to stop there, however, and the mire-like ground conditions which hindered Napoleon en route to defeat at Waterloo, have been attributed to unseasonably heavy rains caused by changing weather patterns wrought by the huge quantities of ash and sulphur aerosols ejected into the atmosphere by the eruption. Mid-year snows and frosts in both Europe and North America ensured that the following year, 1816, was labelled the 'Year without a Summer', and the appalling weather conditions are reported by some to have set the mood for Mary Shelley to pen Frankenstein. At the same time, the extraordinarily brilliant sunsets may also have proved the inspiration for Turner's most colourful works.

As Tambora exploded with 10 times the power of Krakatoa, so the gigantic blast which created Lake Toba in Sumatra around 74,000 years ago was an order of magnitude greater again. One of the greatest eruptions ever known, the 2,200cu km (3 million cu yd) of pulverised rock and gases pumped into the atmosphere lowered temperatures by as much as 15°C (60°F) in some regions, and may well have proved the final straw which plunged an already cooling planet into the icy grip of the glaciers.

While the 18th and 19th centuries were dominated by the great Indonesian eruptions, the biggest and most spectacular events of the last hundred years have occurred further eastward. Two of these, Bezymianny and Tolbachik, lie only a few tens of kilometres apart in the Kamchatka peninsula of Russia, but produced dramatically different eruptions. During 1956 — in a near carbon-copy of the Mt St. Helens eruption 24 years later (see pages 100-101) — part of the

RIGHT: Debris avalanches and lahars have posed the greatest hazard to villagers around Semeru in Eastern Java.

flank of Bezymianny collapsed to form a gigantic landslide that reached over 22km (14 miles) from the volcano, releasing a directed blast which devastated over 500sq km (195sq miles) of forest. In sharp contrast, 20 years later, a giant fissure system opened up near the Tolbachik volcano which spewed out nearly 2sq km (0.75sq miles) of lava to bury an enormous area of the surrounding countryside. Coming further up to date, 1991 proved to be a significant year for Asian volcanoes, with the month of June seeing the climax of one of the biggest eruptions of the 20th century, at Pinatubo in the Philippines, together with the sad deaths of three volcanologists (including Maurice and Katja Krafft, the French volcanologists) during observations of pyroclastic flows at Mt. Unzen (Japan).

While Unzen reinforced the awful dangers faced by volcanologists, 12 of whom have been killed over the past six years, Pinatubo provided the volcano watchers with their best view yet of a major eruption. Not having erupted during historic times, and with no monitoring being undertaken, little was known about how Pinatubo would behave when it reawakened. Both scientists and the local population were to find out, however, when, only 10 weeks after the first rumblings in April, a series of enormous explosions began. These culminated on 15 June with a cataclysmic event which ejected 7cu km (10,000sq yd) of magma and rock, leaving a new 2km (1.25 mile) diameter crater and blanketing an area of over 100sq km (40sq miles) in pyroclastic flows and thick ash deposits. Fortunately,

Loose ash deposited during Pinatubo's 1991 eruption has since provided a ready source of material for lahars during the rainy season. Each mudflow may leave deposits metres thick (BELOW RIGHT) and old river valleys can rapidly be filled (ABOVE RIGHT and BELOW). Settlements around the volcano remain under threat even six years after the eruption.

over a quarter of a million people had been evacuated from the danger zone, so a potential disaster was averted. The eruption did, however, cause great hardship, with several hundred deaths resulting from roofs collapsing under the weight of accumulating ash, and from lahars generated when Typhoon Yunya dumped its load of torrential rain on the great piles of loose ash carpeting the region.

An important lesson Pinatubo has to teach us is that problems with volcanoes don't stop when the eruptions do. Even today the enormous quantities of ash dumped on the flanks of the volcano continue to be converted to rivers of mud by seasonal rains; clogging rivers, flooding the surrounding towns and farmland, and damaging coastal fisheries. This is tremendous strain on the economy of a developing world country which, in the case of the Philippines, is liable to continue into to the early years of the next millenium.

Merapi – Magic and Volcanology

Indonesia has the highest concentration of active volcanoes in the world, with more than 160 regularly erupting. Merapi is one of those that is perpetually active; its eruptions are always violent and deadly. A million and a half people live in the area of the volcano, and 500.000 of them are threatened directly by any future large scale eruption. However, for now everyone stays, as the land around Merapi is extraordinarily fertile, enriched by each explosion with volcanic dust, a natural, renewable fertiliser — the rice paddies at the foot of the volcano yield three harvests a year.

Pak Marjo is small humorous gentleman, always smiling. He lives in the village of Turgo, on the highest farm up the flanks of the volcano. His body carries the scars of severe burns. Two years ago, a scorching cloud unfurling from Merapi surprised him on the slopes of the volcano, the wind of burning gasses covered more than 300m (1,000ft). The same cloud destroyed his village and killed 40 inhabitants. After three months spent in hospital, Marjo returned to the now evacuated zone and rebuilt his house. When we asked him if he did not fear future eruptions he told us that once already he got out alive, that his life was here, and that life is placed under the protection of Sri Sultan Hamengku Buwono.

For the Javanese the axis of the world passes through Kraton, the sultan's palace, it is here that the forces of good and evil balance , and those of life and death . . . and the sultan is the beam of the balance.

Nobody in Yogjakarta would ever think of upsetting this balance between a volcano and a sultan, the latter the impartial protector of men. The sultan is always appealed to following a renewed eruption, and his intercession can calm the fury of the volcano. His father, the ninth Sultan, isn't he famous for having saved the villages threatened by lahars, destructive mudslides?

The present sultan, a young man, is the upholder of tradition, but also has the will to bring Java into the modern world. He prays and meditates always facing Merapi, but he also pays careful attention to the state of the volcano and is attentive to the opinions given by the vulcanologists.

The present state of the volcano is threatening, and it is probably heading for a resurgence of activity.

On arrival at the summit, one sees the problem immediately — the dome is bigger than ever. Gravitational collapses are constant — more than 80 a day, each one throwing many huge lumps of molten lava down the slopes. But the main fear is a massive rupture of the dome that could generate pyroclastic flows. The actual configuration of the dome makes these fears extremely likely.

In such a situation, continuous surveillance of the volcano is of vital importance. The Indonesian vulcanologists have developed a double local network. All around the base of the volcano can be found a series of observatories which collate the ground measurements. On the volcano itself is a network of automated points around the crater that transmit their readings by radio. The parameters measured are essentially seismic and ground deformation. Seismic waves are good indicators of the level of magma inside the volcano. But this mountain of magma also deforms the whole volacanic structure, and this is recorded at the incline-measuring bases. Other bases watch the flanks of the volcano, which could break open under pressure from the dome growing inside the crater. Finally, surveillance missions are mounted up to the crater to analyse the high-temperature magma gasses, and follow the development of the dome, trying to estimate the risk of destability.

In the face of such peril we hope the god of the volcano will be merciful, and that before a future eruption, he will send clear signals to the vulcanologists so they can provide for the safety of the population.

LEFT: Villagers live under the threatening face of Merapi, enjoying the fertile soil but fearful of an eruption.

BELOW: Monitoring stations should provide a forecast of eruptions.

RIGHT: Collapses from a lava dome brighten the night.

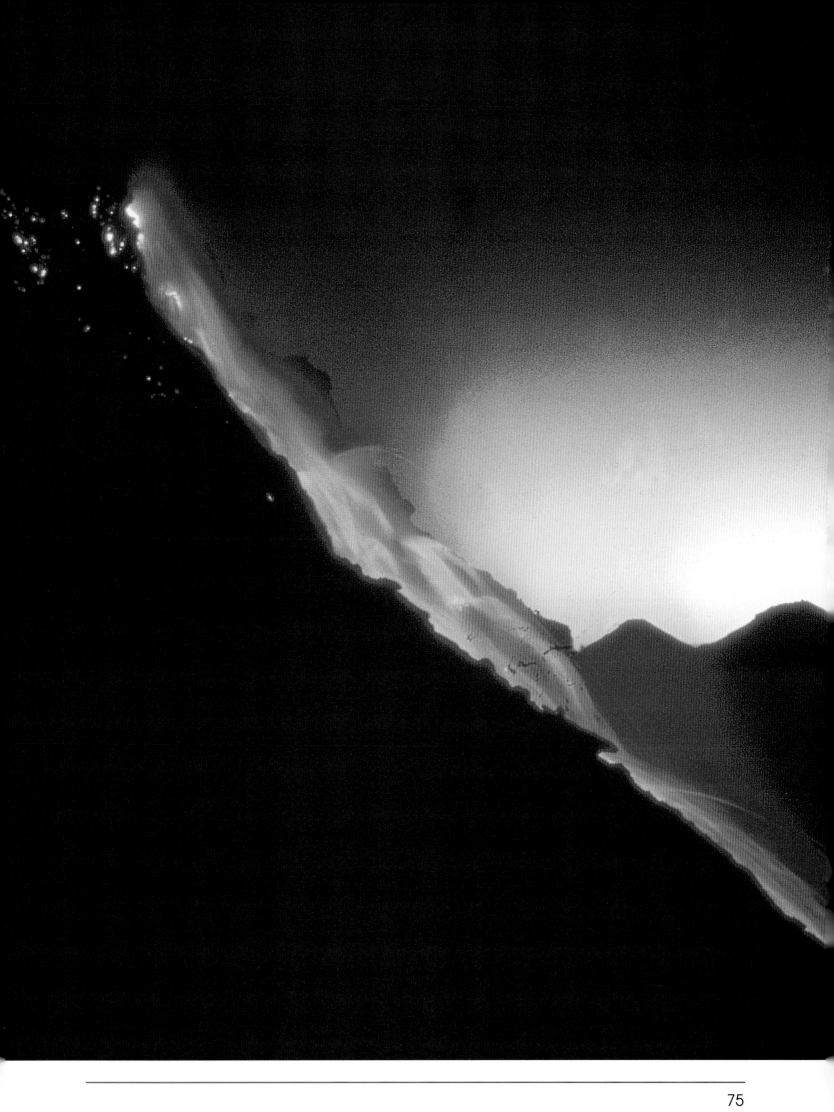

Mount Pinatubo

In the eyes of the witnesses there is no panic, just total shock, as if the fundamental laws of life have been called into doubt. Around us, nothing human remains: a country of phantoms, a countryside with no colour. Uniformly gray. The shapes are still there but they have been softened, and all covered in gray. There is no daylight, just darkness — as if the sky were closing down on us.

It is 14.00hrs on 22 June 1991 and we are in the eighth day of the eruption of Mt Pinatubo

It's raining. It's raining gray; it's raining pulverised rock. Above our heads, an enormous cloud 17,000m (55,750ft) tall fills the sky and blocks all the light. The fine ashes fall, covering everything; slowly, insidiously. We are watching a slow suffocation, a complete obliteration of life. It's a progressive disappearance, as if organic life were slowly changing to mineral. And in the same way as the light has faded, so has all sound disappeared. There's not a whisper, not a sound: men and animals move like ghosts.

Further on, at the heart of the evacuated zone, we reach an old village. It's like a theatre set: houses, beds, tables and chairs, pots and pans . . . everything is there, waiting for the actors. This impression of unreality is underlined by the absence of color. The village is covered under a thick shroud of white ashes. But there is still something more terrible: under the shroud, it has been carbonised!

Devastating pyroclastic flows ran down the side of Pinatubo and one of them stopped a few hundred metres from here. The village felt the heat of the boiling clouds which burned everything. There's not a hint of green: the heads of the palm trees are deformed by the weight of ashes and are dessicated, roasted by the breath of the volcano. And in the houses, the plastic cups and plates have melted on the shelves.

After five days of prudent approach and reconnaissance, we were at last able to see the volcano — from a helicopter, the only way of getting over the area of destruction. From the air we could see the full extent of the devastation. The volcano seemed to have been decapitated: the crater was almost 2km (1.25 miles) wide — double its pre-eruption size. From the crater a phenomenal column of ash and hot gases issued. Enormous rounded billows swelled; a moving and impenetrable wall rose before us. The measurements taken by satellite this morning told us that it was more than 15,000m (49,000ft — nearly ten miles) in height. There was no gap or pause in this, just the continuous expulsion of ash. The continuousness of it all made it seem more impressive: implacable and infinite.

September 1991: the eruption suddenly stopped and no more material issued from the crater. We returned to the volcano on foot, hoping to be able to get close.

A reconnaissance by helicopter showed us a strange countryside: for a distance of several kilometres all around the volcano everything was covered in deep ash. It lay in layers, metres thick, which have filled the valleys and hidden the rivers. A new ground surface had been been produced and already the face of it had started to weather. It had rained a lot these last few weeks and the flow of water traced a new hydrographic network in the marble ashes. The myriad small streams looked like the twigs and

ABOVE: Pinatubo's legacy — a new landscape.

RIGHT: Pinatubo crater — 'We were surprised to discover, at its centre, an emerald lake. Rainwater had accumulated here and the volcanic gases had dissolved into it, transforming the lake from water to hot acid.'

branches of a tree and carried the water to deep canyons which carved notches in the new earth.

Further on, a cloud of steam rose from the new crater. We were surprised to discover, at its centre, an emerald lake. Rainwater had accumulated here and the volcanic gases had dissolved into it, transforming the lake from water to hot acid.

The first party was dropped at the bottom of the crater — the first people to set foot there — and we crossed over the acid lake in a small inflatable boat to sample gases from the on the other side. And so the new crater enters the history of man. It is explored, surveyed, measured, studied . . . until the next eruption.

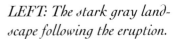
LEFT: The stark gray landscape following the eruption.

CENTER LEFT: Water begins to make its marks in the new landscape.

BOTTOM LEFT: The eruption at Pinatubo killed 800 people with mudflows and pyroclastic flows.

RIGHT: A man tries desperately to remove enough ash from the roof of his house to stop it collapsing from the weight.

Mount Bromo

A sea of sand — flat and empty, like an endless desert disappearing towards the horizon. The only difference between a desert like that and the one I can see, is that here the sand is black and occupies the bottom of a vast depression enclosed by a high wall. In front of us a large volcanic vent lets out a column of white smoke: I'm looking at the volcano Bromo. Two small black points appear like a mirage; two human silhouettes which slowly advance.

Sujahi tells me, "You see, they come from far off. Everyone will come. They will come from each of the villages of Tengger and tomorrow night there will be more than 100,000 for the festival. We should go as well, but before anything else we have to prepare our offerings . . ."

Sujahi is the principal priest of Tengger, a sort of local pope. I have known him for many years and it is entirely because of him that we are here: he has allowed us to follow the Festival of Kesodo at his side and at the side of his faithful followers.

He tells me the story of Tengger and its inhabitants: "The Mojopahit king and his people fled before the arrival of Islam; he left the centre of Java to go east. While traveling they came across a huge mountain: the soil was fertile, there was water and nobody else was living there. We therefore surmounted the ridges and valleys and settled in a sheltered place where we could carry on our traditions without anyone coming to disturb us. Our people were ruled by the Prince Joko Senger and the princess Roro Anteng: the name of our country comes from the contraction of their two names, Teng-Ger. They loved each other but were very unhappy because they could not have children. One day, they were in a grotto on Mont Panenjakan when the creator god Hyang Wide (Brahma to the Hindu) appeared before them. He promised them 25 children on the condition that they offered him the firstborn, to serve him.

"Of course, they made the promise and they started bearing children. Happiness ensued for their family and the whole region. The children grew and the firstborn, Raden Kusuma, was certainly their favorite. The more time passed, the more they forgot their promise and they could not bring themselves to sacrifice their son.

"But the god's patience was running out . . . Soon a series of disasters came down upon the region: first a drought, then the volcano Bromo started erupting ashes. Everywhere they went, the prince, the princess and their children were followed by the wrath of the gods. The princely family ran from hiding place to hiding place but one day as they passed by the foot of the volcano, fire came out of the crater and engulfed Raden Kusuma. Before being dragged to the bottom of the crater, the young prince asked the people to make offerings every year to the god who lived in the volcano. They should be made in memory of him so that disasters should not happen again in the region.

"And every year since then, the inhabitants of Tengger come to pray and make their offerings to the god who lives in the crater so that peace, happiness and prosperity will always reign in our region. We also do it because we are still subjects of the Mojopahit king. Yes, we are the last of the Mojopahits . . ."

The path that leads to the summit of the volcano is very tough going, rising steeply from the sea of sand. Now, as it joins the main cone of the main volcano, it climbs almost vertically — so much so that it has been necessary to cut steps into the last 200m (650ft). Today, they are very crowded steps: two flights of them directing a continuous flow of people up one side and down the other. At the summit we come out onto a narrow ridge, not more than three or four metres (10–13ft) wide: on one side the slope of the cone of the volcano and on the other side the wall of the crater, almost 300m (nearly 1,000ft) down to the active mouths of the volcano. These are swathed in smoke and emit clouds of gas and of water vapor several hundred metres high.

Several hundred people jostle on the edge, trying to find a small flat space which is not too crowded. Each has to

unroll a mat, give the offerings, light a charcoal fire and burn incense. All the gestures are graceful and elegant. As they pray, flower petals are held at the forehead between the fingers of both hands. At the end of the prayer, the petals are thrown in an elegant arc towards the crater, like a message flung to the gods. This is repeated many times, an indication of the intensity of thought that goes into choosing the right offerings to serve as the basis of the prayer. The prayers finished, the sacred atmosphere lifts and it is with laughter that the principal offerings are thrown into the crater.

But as they are thrown, arms emerge from the crater and grab the offerings in mid-flight. Could it be Raden Kusuma coming in person to get what is owed to him? I approach the edge of the ridge and look over. There are people below — jumping, running, climbing and descending as soon as an important offering is thrown from the ridge. They are not there to pray: they are there to recover. There are almost a hundred of them. The contrast between their movement and energy and the calm of the ridge is total.

The pilgrims don't seem troubled that their offerings have fallen into these hands. Smiling, they explain to me that the people taking the offerings come from the low plains of Java — Moslems, who do not believe in ancient gods and see the offerings as bounty with no religious value. Others are also the poor people of the region looking for food. Does it matter? No, of course not: the important thing is the action of the sacrifice: the god will take what he likes.

PREVIOUS PAGES:
ABOVE LEFT: Pilgrims silhouetted against the rim of Bromo.
ABOVE RIGHT: It is important that offerings are carefully prepared for the festival.
BELOW: The volcanic landscape of Tengger. Just how long the offerings to Raden Kusuma will keep the volcano peaceful remains to be seen!

THIS PAGE:
ABOVE RIGHT: Evening falls over Bromo.
FAR RIGHT: The village seen from the air.
CENTER RIGHT: Pilgrims struggle to the rim of the crater.
RIGHT: Procession before the festival.

AUSTRALASIA AND
ANTARCTICA

Throughout history, volcanoes and legend have gone hand in hand, and never more so than in New Zealand where to the aboriginal peoples — the Maori — all volcanoes were gods, and anyone who suffered as a result of their anger must have done something to deserve the doom and destruction vested upon them. Even as recently as the end of the 19th century, such a philosophy held sway, and the destruction of villages by the 1886 eruption of Tarawera was explained away either by the inhabitants eating wild honey (a taboo of the Maori religion) — a clear case of sugar being bad for your health — or due to their having been contaminated by contact with the European settlers.

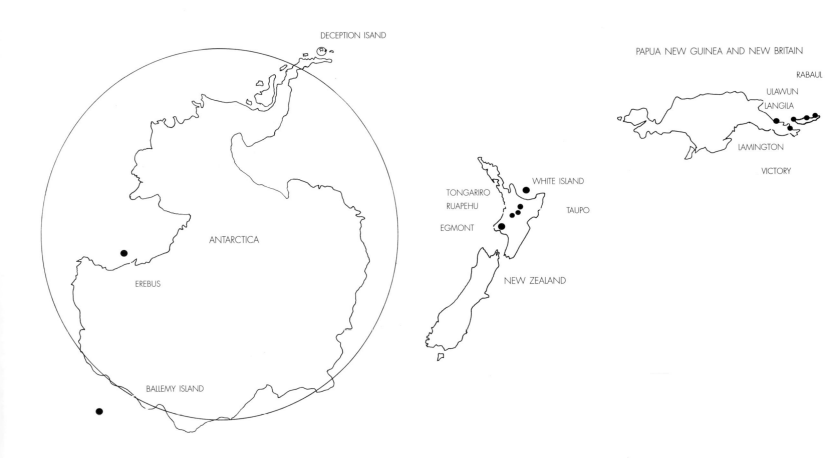

DECEPTION ISAND

PAPUA NEW GUINEA AND NEW BRITAIN

RABAUL

ULAWUN

LANGILA

LAMINGTON

VICTORY

WHITE ISLAND

TONGARIRO
RUAPEHU

TAUPO

EGMONT

ANTARCTICA

NEW ZEALAND

EREBUS

BALLEMY ISLAND

The Maori attached human emotions to their volcanoes, sometimes interpreting eruptions in terms of violent arguments triggered by passion or jealousy between neighbouring volcanoes. Two of New Zealand's most active volcanoes, Mount Egmont and Ruapehu, are said, for example, to have fought fo the love of a third (presumably female?) volcano, Tongariro. In the ensuing battles, Ruapehu poured boiling waters from his crater lake while Egmont destroyed the summit of Ruapehu with a rain of huge blocks. At the climax, Ruapehu spat molten rock at Egmont who fled, burning and defeated to the sea. Although we now treat such tales as reflecting a combination of primitive superstition and ignorance, they did serve an important purpose at the time. When knowledge was handed down largely by word of mouth, they ensured that generations maintained a wariness of potentially-dangerous volcanoes, and even now the Maoris avoid living within range of Ruapehu or Egmont.

VOLCANO LOG: AUSTRALASIA AND ANTARCTICA
Active volcanoes and volcanic fields

Antarctica	23
Australia	1
New Zealand	20
Papua New Guinea and neighbouring islands	58
South Sandwich Islands	8
Solomon Islands and Vanuatu	29
Tonga, Fiji, and neighbouring islands	26
Total	165

The biggest and the deadliest

Volcano	Eruption	Vol (cu km) erupted	Casualties
Kuwae (Vanuatu)	1425	10	many **P**
Lamington (PNG)	1951	0.1	2,942 **P**
Long Island (PNG)	1660	10	2,000 **PFT**
Manam (PNG)	1996	?	Few **P**
Rabaul (PNG)	1937	0.1	507 **P A**
	1850	?	Many **A**
Ritter (PNG)	1888	?	3,000 **L T**
Ruapehu (NZ)	1953	no eruption	151 **M**
Savo (Solomon Is.)	1840	small	many **A P**
Tarawera (NZ)	1886	2	153 **A**
Taupo (NZ)	1846	no eruption	66 **L**
Tinakula (Solomon Is.)	1840	small	many **P**

Key: **A**=ash fall and/or falling blocks **D**=disease **F**=famine **G**=gases **L**=landslides **La**=lavas **M**=mudflows **P**=pyroclastic flows **T**=tsunami

Personal Experiences
A volcanologist's life is not only often dangerous, but frequently without the creature-comforts which most of us come to expect. In a fax to one of the authors (Bill McGuire) of this book, volcanologist Steve Saunders reports on conditions in Rabaul Town in Papua New Guinea as the 1994 eruption continues into 1996.

'Although I hope to get an e-mail link in the New Year, I will probably have to fund it myself from home. The Observatory only has two phone lines, one phone and one fax, and there is no money to pay the phone bill. The phone company would cut us off, but you can imagine the media response if the volcano observatory was reduced to using runners and carrier pigeons. Its Sunday morning and there is thunder rolling outside, so it is quite dark, the electricity and water are off, and I am hot, sticky, and because of the eruption, dirty. I would give a fortune for a bath right now. There is the occasional earth tremor, and if I was in London I would think it was a lorry going by. I will have to finish now as the battery on the computer is running low . . . it is now six hours later and the electricity has come back on so I have been able to put the paraffin lamp out . . . hurrah!'

Clearly, then, the stories constituted an early but effective volcanic hazard mitigation policy.

Like Iceland, New Zealand is a land of fire and ice, although unlike its north Atlantic equivalent, the two elements are largely segregated, with the active volcanoes confined to the warmer North Island. Many of New Zealand's volcanoes are characterised by sticky, gas-rich, rhyolitic which erupt with great violence, and no other country has experienced so many giant eruptions since the ice age. In many cases, eruptions involve the expulsion of enormous pyroclastic flows which cover thousands of square kilometres, accompanied by collapse of the volcano to form a caldera. One such event, that occurred only around 1,800 years ago, may have been one of the most powerful eruptions ever recorded, and it devastated the countryside around Lake Taupo, a region now heavily populated. A similar-sized eruption today is by no means impossible, and would have catastrophic consequences for much of the North Island and its people.

More recently, New Zealand volcanoes have continued to explode into life with varying degrees of violence. In 1886 a 16km (10 mile) long fissure opened suddenly in the Taupo region at the aforementioned Tarawera, sending a cloud of ash up to a height of nearly 10km (6 miles) — unusual for a basaltic eruption which is not normally so explosive. Although incredibly violent, the eruption only lasted for only a few hours, but in this time three villages were buried and more than 100 inhabitants killed.

Volcanoes do not need to be in eruption to cause death and destruction, as evidenced by the Ruapehu disaster of 1953. Here, a barrier of ash which acted as a dam for a crater lake gave way suddenly and sent millions of gallons of water flooding down valleys draining the volcano. The water rapidly mixed with soil and other debris to form mudflows which destroyed the Tangiwai bridge just before the arrival of the Wellington-Aukland express. With no warning and no time to stop, the engine and its five carriages plunged into a ravine killing over 150 people.

Ruapehu continues to pose a problem to its local inhabitants and to those who ski regularly on its slopes, and during the most recent eruption in 1995, mudflows continued to cause difficulties.

The volcanoes of New Zealand form part of two chains, one of which extend northwestwards into the islands of Vanuatu and the Solomon Islands, and the other northeastwards towards Fiji, Tonga, and Samoa. Although some major death-dealing eruptions are recorded in Vanuatu and the Solomon Islands, no major disaster has yet impinged upon the tropical paradises of Fiji, Tonga, and Samoa — at least during historic times — the only shadows being cast by the deaths of around 40 people during two 19th century eruptions

Clouds of steam by day (ABOVE RIGHT) are illuminated at night by lava (BELOW RIGHT) in the Ketetahi vents, near Ngauruhoe, in the Tongariro National Park on North Island.

ABOVE: Looking down from Ruapehu onto Ngauruhoe, the third highest peak on North Island. Until a lull since1977, the volcano commonly erupted every few years.

FAR RIGHT: Ruapehu is the highest peak on the North Island of New Zealand. Between bouts of eruptive activity, the thick snow refills the summit crater lake and provides ideal skiing conditions (BELOW RIGHT) with Ngauruhoe in the distance.

of Niuafo'ou volcano in Tonga. South of New Zealand lies the huge, still largely virgin, continent of Antarctica; another world of ice and fire. Here, although they pose little threat to humans, volcanoes continue to rumble on, and Erebus — the greatest of the volcanoes in this snowy wastes — has erupted a dozen times this century alone.

Unlike New Zealand and its neighbouring island archipelagos, Australia is rarely associated with volcanic activity. The continent is not, however, completely free of the threat, and the most recent eruption — in the far southeast of the country — is less than 3,000 years old. This is no time at all as far as a volcano is concerned, and there is no reason why fresh magma should not breach the surface once again in this region.

In sharp contrast to Australia, Papua New Guinea to the north is a hot-bed of volcanic activity, with — rather like the Kamchatkan peninsula of Russia (see pages 68 and 70) several volcanoes often erupting simultaneously. Lamington, Rabaul, Manam, Long Island, Ritter, Tinakula, and Savo have all brought death to the people living on their slopes, with Manam taking a number of lives due to pyroclastic flows as recently as 1996.

The 1951 eruption of Mount Lamington is one of the best documented of the PNG eruptions, largely through the efforts of the Australian volcanologist G. A. M. Taylor. Prior to the eruption, Lamington was thought to be extinct, sadly a common assumption where a volcano has not erupted within living memory. The onset of increasingly more violent earthquakes during January 1951, often accompanied by landslides on the volcano's flanks, hinted, however, that the assumption was far correct, and this was confirmed when 'smoke' was observed rising from the crater. Soon ash began to be ejected, and dark clouds wracked by lightning rose to heights of 10km (6 miles) or more. At 10.40am on the morning of 21 January disaster struck as a giant black cloud spread like a great mushroom from the summit and pyroclastic flows rolled down the flanks on all sides. Neither the local villagers nor the workers in the sugar cane plantations had any notion of what to expect; neither had they a chance to escape. Within minutes — as at St. Pierre and St. Vincent in the Caribbean (see page 124 onward) over nearly 3,000 people had died in the most hideous manner imaginable.

Papua New Guinea's most famous volcano is probably Rabaul on the island of New Britain. Like Yellowstone and Long Valley in the United States (see page 101) and Campi Flegrei in Italy (see pages 28 and 32), Rabaul is a restless caldera; a giant volcanic crater formed in past times, which continues to swell and subside as fresh magma rises beneath it, and which experiences regular swarms of earthquakes. In contrast to the American and European examples, however, Rabaul remains very active and very dangerous, killing

many inhabitants in 1850 and again in 1937. During the mid-1980s, the staff of the Rabaul Volcano Observatory became increasingly worried by inceasing numbers of earthquakes and by the swelling of the central part of the caldera. The local people were placed on alert and trained in how to respond if an eruption should start. Although the situation had returned to normal by 1985, these initiatives did eventually bear fruit. In September 1994, after only 27 hours of seismic activity, explosive eruptions began simultaneously at two volcanoes on either side of the caldera — Vulcan and Tavurvur. As well as an 18km (11 miles) high ash cloud, the area was also affected by pyroclastic flows and lava flows, and town of Rabaul suffered heavy damage, mainly from the heavy ash fall. Fortunately there were very few casualties, for the local people remembered their training and evacuated the town rapidly and efficiently before the eruption took hold — a real success story for the staff of the Volcano Observatory and a lesson in how important and effective education and training are to preventing volcanic disasters.

Mt Erebus, on Ross Island in Antarctica, is the world's most southerly volcano. Named after the Greek god of darkness, a lava lake is commonly present within the volcano's summit, sending columns of steam skyward (BELOW). Steam escapes from fumaroles on the crater rim (FAR LEFT) and frequently obscures the bottom of the crater (OVERLEAF). One of the early tests for a robot designed to explore Mars was to descend the crater, but the attempt was only partially successful. On 27 November 1979, an Air New Zealand DC-10 crashed into the volcano while commemorating the 50th anniversary of Richard Byrd's pioneering flight over the South Pole. All aboard were killed.

NORTH AMERICA

On 3 June 1912 Katmai village was a remote and unhurried set-tlement in the wilds of Alaska. On 6 June, it made history as the village that looked into hell and survived. After two days of earthquakes — unusual, but not unheard of on the Alaskan penin-sula — a black cloud settled over at least 10,000sq km (2.5 million acres), removing all traces of sunlight for almost three days. Noxious gases filled the atmosphere and acidic rain burned holes in clothing and attacked the skin of those venturing outside. 'We are awaiting death at any moment.' Wrote Ivan Orloff, trapped at near-by Kaflia Bay. 'We cannot see the daylight. We have no water, the rivers are just ashes mixed with water. Here are darkness and hell, thunder and noise. I do not know whether it is day or night. The

ALEUTIAN Is.
PARLOF
REDOUBT
SPURR
VENIAMINOF
AUGUSTINE
EDZIZA
TSEAX RIVER CONE
BAKER
RANIER
St. HELENS
HOOD
YELLOWSTONE
MAMMOTH CRATER (MEDICINE LAKE)
SHASTA
LASSEN PEAK

earth is trembling, it lightens every minute. It is terrible. We are praying.' And, indeed, pray they might, caught as they were in the world's largest eruption this century.

Just 60km (40 miles) from Kaflia Bay, new vents had opened among volcanoes previously considered extinct. Following a landslide from the aptly-named Falling Mountain, adjacent Novarupta burst into life with explosions that were heard up to 1,400km (870 miles) away. Within 60 hours, the volcano had expelled some 30 cu km (1.2 million cu yd) of ignimbrite and ashes, draining magma also from neighbouring Mount Katmai, 10km (6 miles) further west, whose unsupported summit collapsed by 250m (820ft), forming also a caldera whose greatest depth exceeds a kilometre.

Much of the material flowed as an ignimbrite into the valley below Novarupta and Falling Mountain. An expedition arriving four years later found the deposits still hot enough to vaporise water, so that the valley seemed to be filled with tens of thousands of steaming columns, 'as though all the steam engines in the world, assembled together, had popped their safety valves at once and were letting off steam in concert.' Today, only a few wisps remain to keep alive the memory of the Valley of Ten Thousand Smokes.

Novarupta is one of almost 100 active volcanoes stretching from the Canadian border west through the Alaskan Peninsula and along the Aleutian Arc, 2,500km (1,500 miles) of islands that stretch more than half way across the North Pacific towards Russia's

VOLCANO LOG: NORTH AMERICA
Active volcanoes and volcanic fields

Canada	20
United States (Alaska)	94
United States (West Coast)	51
United States (Interior)	20
Total	185

The biggest and the deadliest

Volcano	Eruption	Vol (cu km) erupted	Casualties
Crater Lake (US)	2900BC	100	—
Novarupta (US)	1912	10	few ?
Mt St. Helens (US)	1980	2	57 **PLM**
Redoubt (US)	1989	0.001	—
Spurr (US)	1992	0.001	—
Lassen Peak (US)	1914	?	—

Key: **A**=ash fall and/or falling blocks **D**=disease **F**=famine **G**=gases **L**=landslides **La**=lavas **M**=mudflows **P**=pyroclastic flows **T**=tsunami

Personal Experiences
In June 1912, Captain Perry of the US Coastguard cutter *Manning* observed the eruption of Novarupta from a distance of over 150km (90 miles). Despite the distance, the experience was awful. *All streams and wells have now become chocked, about five inches of ash having fallen, and water was furnished inhabitants by the Manning and by a schooner. At noon, ashes began to fall again, increased until 1.00pm; visibility was about fifty feet. Abject terror took possession of the place. At 2.00pm pitch darkness shut in. There were heavy static disturbances to the radio. No light appeared at dawn on June 8th. Ash had been removed from the ship on June 7th, but now decks, masts, yards, and lifeboats were loaded with flakes of fine dust of a yellowish colour. Sulphurous fumes came at times in the air. Avalanches of ashes could be heard sliding on the neighbouring hills sending forth clouds of suffocating dust. The crew kept at work with shovels, and four streams of water were kept playing incessantly to try to rid the ship of ash. The dust fell so heavily that a lantern could not be seen at arm's length.*

NORTH AMERICA

ABOVE: Mammoth Mountain is a dome in California's Long Valley, a caldera which formed some 700,000 years ago. Recent unrest within the caldera has raised fears of a build-up to another eruption, providing inspiration for the film Dante's Peak.

RIGHT: The 18 May 1980 eruption of Mt St. Helens marked the first volcanic activity in the continental United States for almost seventy years. A landslide exposed pressurized magma within the volcano, triggering a massive blast and pyroclastic flows that devastated more than 600sq km (232sq miles).

Kamchatkan volcanoes (see pages 68 and 70). When the US government bought Alaska from Russia in 1867 for little more than $7 million, it had no idea that it had just acquired North America's most active volcanic state.

Although Alaska and the Aleutians are sparsely populated, and famously bad weather can allow eruptions to pass unseen by even modern satellites, several eruptions are expected in the region each year. Many of these are explosive (such as Augustine in 1986, Redoubt in 1989, and Spurr in 1992), releasing substantial columns of ash high into the atmosphere, right into the flight paths for commercial intercontinental jets. At night or in cloudy weather, it is often not easy for aircraft instruments to recognise a volcanic plume before the plane is surrounded and the ash crazes the windshield and melts inside the engines to choke the turbines. Once caught in a plume, a pilot remarked, the sky soon becomes as 'black as a badger's bottom'; the only response is to drop out of the plume and hope that the engines clear by themselves. On 15 December 1989, a jumbo jet coming to land at Anchorage airport lost power to all four engines because of ash from Redoubt, 200km (125 miles) away. It landed safely, but provided a timely example of how today's technology remains vulnerable to the whims of nature.

Next door to Alaska, the Yukon and British Columbia are famous in folk memory for the gold rush, but not for volcanic eruptions. Yet 20 active volcanoes lurk where the ever-hopeful were teased to seek out their fortune. Only two historical eruptions have been recorded, both in British Columbia: along the Tseax River in 1730, and at Ruby Mountain in 1898. However, just 1,200 years ago (more recently, for example, than the destruction of Pompei by Vesuvius in 79 AD), Bona-Churchill (just on the Alaskan side of the border with the Yukon) produced an eruption comparable to that of Novarupta in 1912, while in about 400 BC, Mt Meager unleashed a plinian eruption whose ash settled out as far east as Alberta. Indeed, dated eruptions for the last 10,000 years hint at renewals of activity at intervals of 1,000-2,000 years, so the relative tranquillity in historic times may perhaps be a false calm before a new storm arrives.

South of the Canadian border, the Pacific coast volcanoes follow the trend of the Cascade range from Washington, through Oregon, to North California, with eastward excursions through Idaho to Yellowstone in Wyoming, and also across the more southerly western states. Nearly 50 active centres have been recognised along the Cascades, but only five have erupted since the arrival of European settlers: Mts. Baker, St. Helens, Hood, and Shasta, as well as Lassen Peak. Of these, only Lassen Peak and Mount St. Helens have had confirmed eruptions this century.

Located in the southern Cascades, and about 250km (150

PREVIOUS PAGE:
Lassen Peak in California
was thought to be dormant
until 30 May 1914, when it
exploded to life with the first
of a series of eruptions which
continued to 1917.

miles) north of Sacramento, Lassen Peak's last burst of activity coincided almost exactly with the years of the Great War, although without the frightening death toll. Small explosions during 1914 were followed by over 150 explosions over the next 12 months which ejected clouds of ash to heights of 3km (2 miles) or more. The climactic explosion occurred in the spring of the following year, with pyroclastic flows and lahars flattening forests nearly 7km (4 miles) from the summit. The accompanying ash cloud rose to almost 10km (6 miles), and dropped ash over much of western Nevada. Smaller explosions occurred periodically as activity began to die down, and the volcano returned to its slumber during the summer of 1917.

Mt St. Helens had been quiet for over 100 years before it coughed again to life in March 1980. The first eruption in mainland USA during the television era, the reawakening soon caught worldwide media attention, as new magma gradually pushed a bulge 2km (1.2 miles) across the volcano's northern face. The catastrophe arrived six weeks later at 08.32 on 18 May, when an earthquake dislodged the bulging mountainside, releasing the magma pent-up within. With a blast that could be heard 300km (185 miles) away, clouds of ash, old rock and steam were propelled downslope at 300°C (575°F) and hurricane velocities. Nearly 600sq km (230sq miles) were totally devastated, including prime Douglas fir forest, and homes, bridges and roads were demolished by torrents of steaming mud travelling at 50kph (30mph). For several hours the volcano continued to pump ash skywards and layers at least 5cm (2in) thick were deposited 1,000km (600 miles) away in Montana. Altogether, nearly 4cu km (5,250cu yd) of ash and pyroclastic flows were erupted, and the once 2,950m (9,676ft) peak is now 450m (1,476ft) lower and scarred by a crater 2km (1.2 miles) across and 600m (2,280ft) deep. Fifty-seven people died, including volcanologist David Johnston, who was manning the forward monitoring post of the US Geological Survey at the time. Today, the St .Helens' crater is being gradually refilled by a dome of viscous lava and, together with nearby volcanoes in the chain, is under continuous surveillance by the Cascades Volcano Observatory, established after the 1980 eruption.

About 400km (250 miles) south of Mt St. Helens lies the spectacular result of a much bigger bang which shattered the peace of the native American's world. Around 5,000 years ago, a huge explosion caused the collapse of Mt Mazama to form a giant 10km (6 mile) basin which over time filled with water to form Crater Lake. Although no eruption of similar size has occurred over the past few thousand years, the potential always exists for another volcanic catastrophe on the scale of Mt Mazama — or even greater. Most recently, concern has focused on the Long Valley volcanic cen-

OVERLEAF: On 18 May
1980, Mt St. Helens was
decapitated by 450m
(1,500ft), its peak being
replaced by a crater 2km
(1.25 miles) across and over
600m (2,000ft) deep. The pale
areas show part of the region
devastated by the eruption.

tre in northern California, and only about 300km (185 miles) east of San Francisco. Long Valley hosts the famous ski resort of Mammoth Lakes, and constitutes one of North America's two restless calderas; large depressions formed in giant eruptions which are again showing signs of life. Both Long Valley, and the other restless caldera, Yellowstone in Wyoming — home of the Old Faithful geyser — are characterised by episodes of ground swelling and subsidence, often accompanied earthquake activity. At Long Valley, the current period of unrest started in 1980 with swarms of earthquakes and changes in the temperatures and compositions of hot springs and the appearance of new ones. At the same time the ground started to swell, and has now risen by over 0.5m (1.5ft) since the mid-1970s. Dead vegetation also provided testament to the release of carbon dioxide and other noxious gases. Taken together, all these signs can only mean one thing. Fresh magma is nearing the surface, and an eruption may be possible in the near future. Although the caldera itself formed by a gigantic explosion about 700,000 years ago, there have been smaller eruptions in the area much more recently, around six hundred years ago. The threat to the Mammoth Lakes resort and other settlements in the Long Valley area is a real one, and xvolcanologists of the US Geological Survey are keeping a round-the-clock watch on the situation to ensure that no-one has a nasty surprise.

BELOW: Although not normally considered to be a volcanic country, the west coast of Canada contains a string of active volcanoes, including the Garibaldi complex, that connect the Cascade Range in North America to the Alaskan province.

MEXICO AND
CENTRAL AMERICA

Not even paradise is free from eruptions. In the state of Michoacan, half-way between the Pacific and Mexico City, a remote tropical plateau nestles below the snow-capped peaks of the Sierra Madre. Its soils are extremely fertile and, 250 years ago, these provided crops in abundance, from indigo and sugar cane to sweet corn and sorghum. Nobody doubted that the Tarascan indians had wisely named the place Jorullo (or paradise): it was bountiful, it was beautiful, it was peaceful and serene. It was also quite uncompromisingly volcanic.

Early symptoms of unrest came in June 1759, when farmers began talking about strange noises underground. As days turned to weeks, the noises became louder and the ground started to tremble until, on 17 September, the air was filled with shots like cannon fire while strong tremors threatened to bring down the main church. A priest arrived from nearby Patzcuaro to celebrate mass, a strategy

followed 10 days later by a sudden return to tranquillity. Relief swept the plateau, but just as thoughts turned to celebration, the earth tore itself apart.

Before dawn on 29 September, dense steam clouds boiled from new fissures a mere 2–3km (1.2–1.9km) from the principal farms. Mud rained over the countryside, bringing with it the choking stench of sulphur, that clings to lungs and clothes with equal abandon. As the villagers expected certain destruction, it was small consolation that few others have ever witnessed a volcano at birth.

The first stages of the eruption were marked by the expulsion of rock and groundwater ahead of the rising magma. For over a week, much of the old rock was ground into particles and hurled skyward as sticky mud, while nearby streams became flooded, drowning many animals before they could flee. Only on 8 October did new magma break the surface, feeding lava fountains and strombolian explosions which, in less than a month, had produced a scoria cone 250m (820ft) high and about a kilometre across. Shortly afterwards, activity settled down to the more sedate extrusion of basaltic lava flows at about 1,100°C (2,012°F), interrupted by explo-

it covered the sun. By 11, the whole sky was covered, and we were enveloped in the greatest darkness, unable to see even the nearest objects . . . Everything combined to fill the stoutest souls with fear, even more so at 4 o'clock, when the earth began to quake and to continue a perpetual shaking which gradually increased. This was followed by a shower of phosphoric sand until 8 o'clock, when there began a heavy fall of powder-like flour. Thunder and lightning continued the whole night and the following day . . . The darkness lasted 43 hours, and it was indispensible for us to carry a light, even if it was not sufficient to see with . . . From dawn on the 23rd, a dim sunlight showed the uneven streets quite level, being covered with dust. Men, women and children were so disfigured that it was not easy to recognise anyone except by their voices or other circumstances . . . At 10 o'clock we were again plunged into darkness . . . and, though leaving brought immediate peril from wild beasts fleeing the forests, . . . more than half the inhabitants of La Union emigrated on foot, abandoning their houses, well persuaded that they should never return to them.

VOLCANO LOG: CENTRAL AMERICA
Active volcanoes and volcanic fields

Mexico	35
Guatemala	22
El Salvador	18
Honduras	4
Nicaragua	16
Costa Rica	13
Panama	2
Total	110

The biggest and deadliest

VOLCANO	ERUPTION	VOL (cu km) ERUPTED	CASUALTIES
Colima, Mexico	1576	0.03 (?)	Many ?
El Chicon, Mexico	1982	1	2,000 **P**
Santa Maria,	1902	10	6,000 **AG**
Guatemala	1929	?	5,000 (?)**P**
Ilopango, El Salvador	260BC	10 (?)	Thousands ?
Coseguina, Nicaragua	1835	2	Dozens **G?**
Mombacho, Nicaragua	1570	?	400 **L**
Arenal, Costa Rica	1968	?	80 **PA**
Irazu, Costa Rica	1963	0.03 (?)	40 **MA**

Key: **A**=ash fall and/or falling blocks **D**=disease **F**=famine **G**=gases **L**=landslides **La**=lavas **M**=mudflows **P**=pyroclastic flows **T**=tsunami

sive outbursts that built the main cone to 350m (1,150ft) and produced four smaller neighbours. By the end of the eruption in 1774, nearly 2cu km (2,600cu yd) of magma had been expelled and lava flows had buried over 10sq km (4sq miles) of prime land. Gas and steam continued to leak out for more than 150 years, heating thermal springs that became popular for their apparent medicinal relief. Today, Jorullo is again peaceful, but it is the peace of a paradise lost and not yet regained.

Though unnerving to local farmers, eruptions like that at Jorullo are by no means unusual to the Mexican southwest. Across 1,600sq km (620sq miles), more than 150 broadly basaltic scoria cones pepper the foothills of ancient volcanoes, towering overhead to almost 4,000m (13,000ft). Since Jorullo, one more cone has been added, at Paracutin, some 70km (45 miles) to the northwest. Starting in the middle of a cornfield in February 1943, this last eruption continued for nine years, building a cone 360m (1,200ft) tall and spewing lava over 25sq km (6,200 acres. See Personal Experiences on pages 94–95). To see it in eruption, watch the closing scenes of the *Captain from Castile*, a 1947 potboiler with Tyrone Power.

Jorullo and Paracutin have given volcanologists two of the best examples of how volcanoes are born. They also illustrate the curious condition in which eruptions hardly ever occur in the same place twice. The result is an apparent scattering of modest cones and lava flows, rather than the growth of a major basaltic edifice, like Sicily's Mt Etna or Mt Cameroon in West Africa (see pages 32 and 46). It is interesting, though, that volcanoes such as Etna cover 1,000-2,000sq km

RIGHT: Popocatepetl and Ixtaccihuatl overlook the plateau that is now home to Mexico City. Renewed activity at Popocatepetl is currently causing concern among satellite towns and villages.

Personal Experiences

Birth of a volcano. Paracutin, 20 February 1943. Dionisio Pulido, joint owner of the Rancho Tepacua in which Paracutin was formed.

At 4 o'clock I left my wife to set fire to a pile of branches

RIGHT: El Laco is the world's highest volcanic mine. It has erupted lava composed almost entirely of iron ore, creating a unique flow essential to local economies. Miners work in shifts of weeks or more and, when they descend home, they must undergo medical treatment to adjust to the lower altitudes.

BELOW: The cone of Paricutin marks the youngest vent in the Michoacan-Guanajuato volcano field. The eruption continued for nine years, spreading lava over 25 sq km of prime farmland.

(400-800sq miles) at their base, areas similar to that of the Michoacan volcanic field. Moreover, they have been active for hundreds of thousands of years, while the oldest known cones in Michoacan data back to only tens of thousands of years. Perhaps the Michoacan field is not just a random collection of cones, but the foundation of a major volcano that will grow over the next half million years.

Before then, however, plenty of other eruptions will have reshaped the Mexican landscape. Apart from a dozen or so volcanic centres in Baja California (the northwest peninsula pulled away from the mainland), most of Mexico's volcanoes lie in the south, forming a crude east-west belt that incorporates both Guadalajara and Mexico City, together the home for over 23 million people. Historic activity in the west has been dominated by Colima (the 'god of the ruling fires') which, with over 50 eruptions since 1560, is Mexico's most active volcano. At the eastern end lies El Chichon (the 'lump on the head'), which in 1982, exploding after a lull of more than five centuries, killed some 2,000 people and, sending sulphur-rich gases 26km (16 miles) into the stratosphere, created a veil of aerosols that blocked the sun's rays and reduced global temperatures by several tenths of a degree Centigrade. Midway along the belt rises majestic Popocatepetl (the 'smoking mountain'), the second highest peak in Mexico (5,465m/17,925ft) and whose outburst in 1345, witnessed by the Aztecs, marks the earliest volcanic activity recorded in the New World.

Beyond El Chichon, the chain of active volcanoes swings southeast along the Pacific margin of Central America, from Guatemala to Panama. Created by the eastward subduction of the Pacific plate, these volcanoes are renowned for their sudden violence. Two classic examples are Santa Maria, in Guatemala, and Cosegina on the border between Nicaragua and El Salvador.

Rising to 3,768m (12,359ft), Santa Maria before 1902 boasted a near-perfect conical form. It had never rumbled in historic time and, with its forested slopes, was seen as an idyllic backdrop to the coffee plantations of Western Guatemala. On 24 October 1902, the idyll was shattered as the coastal flank of the volcano failed, allowing the explosive release of 10cu km (13,000cu yd) of gas-rich andesite (compare the 1980 eruption of North America's Mt. St. Helens, pages 100–101). The explosion was heard in Costa Rica, 800km (500 miles) distant, while pyroclastic flows decimated the slopes, and columns of ash were buoyed aloft to 30km (18 miles). By the end of the eruption, 300,000sq km (116,000sq miles) had been buried by ash, and the southwest flank of the volcano had become a precipice more than two kilometres deep. Over 1,500 people were killed by toxic gases and by their houses collapsing beneath

which Demetrio and I and another . . . had gathered. I went to burn the branches when I noticed that . . . a fissure had opened, and I saw that this fissure, as I followed it with my eye, was long and passed from where I stood . . . and continued in the direction of the Cerro de Canijuata . . . Here is something new and strange, thought I, and I searched the ground for signs to see whether or not it had opened that night, but could find none . . . I set about to ignite the branches again, when I felt a thunder, the trees trembled, and I turned to speak to Paula; it was then that I saw how the hole in the ground raised and swelled itself, two or two-and-a-half metres [6.5–8ft] high, and a kind of smoke or fine dust, which was grey like ash, began to rise, with a hiss or whistle, loud and continuous, and there was a smell of sulphur . . . I ran to see if I could save my wife and my companions and my oxen, but I could not find them . . . Then, very frightened, I mounted my mare and galloped to Paracutin, where I found my wife and son and friends waiting, fearing that I was dead and that they would never see me again. On the road to Paracutin, I had thought of my little animals, the yoke oxen, that were going to die in the flame and the smoke, but upon arriving at my house I was happy to see that they were there.

accumulated ash; another 3,000 or more perished from malaria, caused by an increase in the number of mosquitoes after their natural predators had been wiped-out by ash. Twenty years later, a dome of viscous andesite emerged into the 1902 crater and has been growing ever since, spasmodically collapsing to trigger pyroclastic flows, one of which killed several hundreds, possibly thousands, of people in 1929.

The reawakening of Santa Maria produced the biggest eruption on record in Mexico and Central America; only the 260 AD eruption of Ilopango in El Salvador has achieved a similar size. It is one of the many examples when a volcano, popularly believed to be extinct and so not properly monitored, comes back to life with an eruption of outstanding proportions.

In much the same way, Coseguina caught populations by surprise in 1835. Despite small eruptions in 1709 and 1809, the volcano was generally held to be extinct by those living around the adjacent Gulf of Fonseca. By local standards, moreover, Coseguina appeared to be quite modest, a truncated cone less than 900m (2,950ft) high: pretty, but not awesome — the exact opposite of its sudden eruption on 20 January 1835. For almost three days, Coseguinan ash blotted out the sun for hundreds of kilometres (see Personal Experience pages 104–105). Its explosions were heard in Jamaica, 1,300km (800 miles) east, and in Bogota (Colombia), 1,800km (1,120 miles) southeast. In Belize, 500km (310 miles) distant, troops were mustered because the detonations were mistaken for enemy cannons, while in Alancho, 150 unwedded couples were frightened into getting married before the Day of Judgement arrived. Not for a long time had priests been so popular.

Since 1835, Coseguina has hiccupped gently only twice, in 1852 and 1859. It was believed for a while that such quiet could be maintained by sacrificing an infant. Old accounts of similar beliefs can be found throughout Mexico and Central America, hardly surprising given the anxiety induced by eruptions from 110 volcanic districts. During the 1880 activity of Ilopango, 160km (100 miles) northwest of Coseguina, sacrifices were proposed to appease the volcano, apparently angered by a new ferry service across its crater lake. In Nicaragua, the indians sacrificed beautiful virgin girls to placate Masaya which, in spite of the strict qualifications required of the candidates, has continued to erupt regularly for at least 450 years. Indeed, Masaya is one of the few volcanoes where more orthodox attempts have also been made to block the main vent and to pipe acidic fumes away from plantations nearby. The attempts were not successful, but the more practical attitude to the volcano does at least allow today's maidens to mature without fear.

ABOVE and RIGHT: Colima is one of Mexico's most active volcanoes. Major prehistoric eruptions triggered landslides that travelled tens of kilometres and buried neighbouring districts under thick ash deposits, including the Pre-Mayan temple seen on the left of the photograph above.

SOUTH AMERICA

Personal Experiences
The eruption of Calbuco, Chile, 6 January 1929. Federico Reichert, who was climbing Derrumbo, a neighbouring peak, when the eruption began.

After setting out downhill at about 7 o'clock in the morning, we found ourselves faced by a strange condition. At first we had the sensation that it was raining, but very quickly found that we were mistaken. We looked up and verified the fact that it was a volcanic eruption, which in my judgement proceeded from the mountain Calbuco, situated some 15–20km [9–12 miles] from the spot . . . Little by little the sky was darkening more. The south cove of Lake Todos los Santos was wrapped in an impenetrable blackness . . . At o'clock we reached our moored boat . . . We rowed 10 minutes and found ourselves in the dark, in the middle of a starless night. Under such conditions like blind men, we kept on rowing, anxious to gain the shore. Ordinarily this could be done in 10 minutes, but we now rowed madly for 10 hours and a

Volcanoes, like sex and money, mix badly with politics. Not that politicians take a blind bit of notice: even Benjamin Disraeli, twice British Prime Minister in the late 19nth century, fell to temptation when he compared his opponents with one of 'those marine landscapes not very unusual on the coasts of South America (where) you behold a range of exhausted volcanoes.' Fortunately for himself, Disraeli's opponents were no better, for none pointed out that he had just made two chronic errors: first, South American volcanoes are among the world's most active and, second, many of those which are exhausted are also the sources of extraordinarily rich mineral deposits — an asset that any Member of Parliament would desire.

From Colombia south to Cape Horn, subduction of the Pacific floor below South America has created among the Andes a chain, 8,000km (5,000 miles) long, of the world's highest volcanoes. Loftiest of all is Ojos del Salado, which looks over the border between Chile and Argentina from 6,880m (22,566ft but, even so, still 2,000m (6,560ft) short of the height of Mt. Everest). Although records of eruptions are scanty before 1800, more than 200 volcanoes are presently considered to be active: called the 'Avenue of Volcanoes' in Ecuador, the chain is in reality a superhighway of eruptions.

In spite of their grandeur, the Andean volcanoes are sparsely populated and so their many spectacular eruptions have had only a small impact on large populations. Beyond 20 or 30 years ago, few details were available even for those volcanoes frequently in eruption, such as Lliama and Villarrica in Chile, both of which have erupted some 50 times since the 17th century.

half. We seemed to navigate in a vacuum. The rain of ash bathed our bodies and faces and hindered our looking upward. The situation became complicated a little later by a phenomenon no less strange. We were wrapped in the 'fire of St. Elmo', produced by the high electric tension. From our clothes and our flesh we gave off sparks, and our heads seemed to be surrounded by aureoles. Suddenly the lightning flashed, followed immediately by thunder. The light of the celestial discharge, however, was not enough to tear the curtain of ash and nocturnal darkness which covered everything. Simultaneously the discharges from our bodies stopped and we found ourselves again in chaos . . . Without warning we reached the shore. To orient ourselves we lit matches and debarked without difficulty. We were absolutely ignorant of the point where we arrived. At last, at 11.30, the sky began to clear and we distinguished smokily some outlines of the vicinity. To our surprise we found that we were scarcely 100m (33ft) from the place where we had set out.

VOLCANO LOG: SOUTH AMERICA
Active volcanoes and volcanic fields

Colombia	15
Ecuador	19
Galapagos Islands	14
Peru	13
Bolivia	25
Agentina	29
Chile	86
Total	201

The biggest and deadliest

VOLCANO	ERUPTION	VOL (cu km) ERUPTED	CASUALTIES
Ruiz, Colombia	1985	0.03	25,000 M
Dona Juana, Colombia	1897	0.3?	55 P
Galeras, Colombia	1993	?	9 A
Guagua Pichincha, Colombia	1993	?	2 A
Cotopaxi, Ecuador	1698	0.1?	Many M
	1877	0.3?	300+ M
Huaynaputina, Peru	1600	20?	1,400 M
Villarrica, Chile	1810 BC	2?	?
	1971	0.01?	15 M
Hudson, Chile	1991	3?	?

Key: **A**=ash fall and/or falling blocks **D**=disease **F**=famine **G**=gases **L**=landslides **La**=lavas **M**=mudflows **P**=pyroclastic flows **T**=tsunami

SOUTH AMERICA

Ironically, it is the smaller eruptions that have proved to be the most lethal. Deadliest of all has been Nevado del Ruiz, South America's most northerly active volcano. Improbably known as the smoking nose, Ruiz trembled in mid-November 1984 for the first time in 70 years. One tremble being much like another, initial concern was soon pacified in surrounding Colombia, especially in the regional capital Manizales, 30km (18 miles) northwest, and in rural Armero on the Lagunillas river valley, whose 50km (30 miles) runs almost top to bottom along the eastern flank of the volcano.

A thriving agricultural centre 45km (28 miles) from Ruiz, Armero was the third settlement in 400 years to have been constructed on the same site. More than 4km (2.5 miles) above, the summit of Ruiz (at 5,389m/17,676ft) is perpetually capped by ice and snow. As a result, the heat from even small eruptions can readily melt huge volumes of water to feed the river valleys. As the torrents mix with volcanic debris and pluck sediment from river beds, they rapidly transform themselves into powerful mudflows (or lahars) that can travel down the volcano at 30–40kph (19–25mph). Once in the foothills, the lahars spread from the valley, flooding the plains to depths of several metres (the height of a small house) before setting like cement. Along the Lagunillas, in particular, lahars had erased entire settlements in 1595 and 1845, accounting for more than 1,500 lives. It was a grim omen for Armero in 1984 and, as it turned out a year later, also an omen grimly ignored.

As weeks turned to months, Ruiz's rumblings became more forthright and, battered by persistent warnings, the authorities began to prepare against a major eruption. But even after a year of anticipation, the volcano was

RIGHT: Lascar volcano in Northern Chile has erupted at intervals of less than 30 years since 1848 when written records began.

ABOVE and BELOW
RIGHT: Tumisa is one of
South America's truly
exhausted volcanoes.
Extensively eroded, it is now
mined for its sulphur deposits.

ready first, on 13 November 1985. At 21.08, after six hours of increasing disturbance, 30 million cubic metres (40 million cu yd) of pyroclastic flows were spewed over the icecap. Although extremely modest in size, they were hotter than 900°C (1,650°F) and, rapidly melting the ice, they sent water into the Lagunillas at 30,000cu m/sec (40,000cu yd) enough in a day to flood by more than 100m (325ft) an area such as central London or downtown Los Angeles). Two hours later, the lahar reached Armero. A wave almost 40m (130ft) high swept through the town, taking over 20,000 victims. Eighty kilometres (50 miles) away, on the other side of Ruiz, 1,800 people were killed in Chinchiná, overwhelmed by mudflows down the volcano's western flank. Altogether, 25,000 people died, 5,000 were injured, and another 10,000 left homeless: the world's fourth most deadly volcanic disaster and the worst since the destruction of St. Pierre, on Martinique, in 1902 (see page 124 onward).

Because of their high altitude, most volcanoes in the Andes have summits above the snowline and so it is not surprising that lahars have been among their most frequent hazards. Ecuador's Cotopaxi is no exception, just 80km (50 miles) from Quito and arguably South America's most famous volcano. Quiet since the 1940s, Cotopaxi had been persistently active for the preceding 250 years, at least five eruptions triggering lahars that travelled tens of kilometres from the summit. The last deadly giant mudflow, on 26 June 1877, reached a village almost 250km (155 miles) distant, descending the volcano at speeds approaching 80kph (50mph).

It seems an unreasonable alliance for magma to use glaciers as agents of destruction. Certainly, this was not a combination perceived for El Misti which, with Chachani and Pichu-Pichu, overlooks Arequipa, the second city in Peru. According to legend, the Sun God defeated the evil spirit in El Misti by plunging its head into a lava flow and then filling the crater with ice. The remedy appears to have calmed the volcano, from which no eruptions have been confirmed for 170 years, but it is unlikely to last and, when the spirit finally does clear its head, it will probably use the ice to sweeten its revenge.

Arequipa itself is regarded as one of the world's most beautiful cities. Also known as the white city (ciudad blanca), Arequipa's attraction derives from the grey-white hue of its traditional building stone — blocks from an ignimbrite covering the plains on which the surrounding volcanoes are built. Sheets of ignimbrite are formed when enormous volumes of magmatic froth (commonly tens to hundreds of cubic kilometres) are expelled as ground-hugging currents. Such sheets are found throughout the Andean chain and, mostly of rhyolitic composition, they have ages typically measured in millions of years. Particularly spectacular is the Cerro Galan ignimbrite in

OVERLEAF: El Misti rising
behind the cathedral tower of
Arequipa, one of the world's
most beautiful cities.

SOUTH AMERICA

Northwest Argentina. Formed 2.6 million years ago, the eruption unleashed 200cu km (300,000cu yd) of ignimbrite to distances of 70km (44 miles), creating a caldera 40km (25 miles) across and over 750m (2,500ft) deep: indeed, so large is the caldera that its true structure was only recognised in the early 1970s from images provided by orbiting spacecraft. Hot springs inside the caldera are now the sole reminder of its activity. It is not certain, though, that the volcano is dead. Ignimbrite eruptions of such large volume tend to recur at intervals of millions of years, so it is possible that Cerro Galan is simply biding its time.

While building stones from ignimbrites are of local importance, the cores of ancient volcanoes in the Andes are of global concern. When too old for magmatic eruptions, volcanoes restrict their activity to the internal circulation of hot fluids. As they circulate, the fluids become highly enriched in valuable elements, from gold, silver and copper to sulphur and selenium, and these can eventually be deposited as concentrated ores. In the 17th century, the sheer volume of silver that was mined from the extinct Bolivian volcano Cerro Negro (near Potosi) served to collapse world prices enough to hasten Spain's decline as a colonial nation. Today, about a quarter of the world's copper comes from Andean volcanoes, which have recently enjoyed yet another renaissance as suppliers of selenium, essential for semiconductors in the computer industry. Just a century after Disraeli had described them as exhausted, the ancient volcanoes of South America are feeding the chips on which the modern world depends.

RIGHT: Ignimbrite sheets fill valleys and cover plateaus across the Andes. They are produced by the most violent eruptions, in which clouds of pulverized magma spew over the ground at hundreds of miles an hour.

Villarrica (CENTER) is one of South America's most active volcanoes. Lahars are frequently triggered by eruptions melting snow and ice, and these have destroyed villages in the last 50 years. Much of the activity consists of strombolian explosions in the summit crater (BELOW RIGHT). The lava fragments (OPPOSITE PAGE BELOW) are at temperatures exceeding 1,050°C (1,922°F).

OPPOSITE PAGE ABOVE: A small gas plume rises over the summit of Lascar in 1989. Preliminary activity before its 1993 eruption was first detected by satellite.

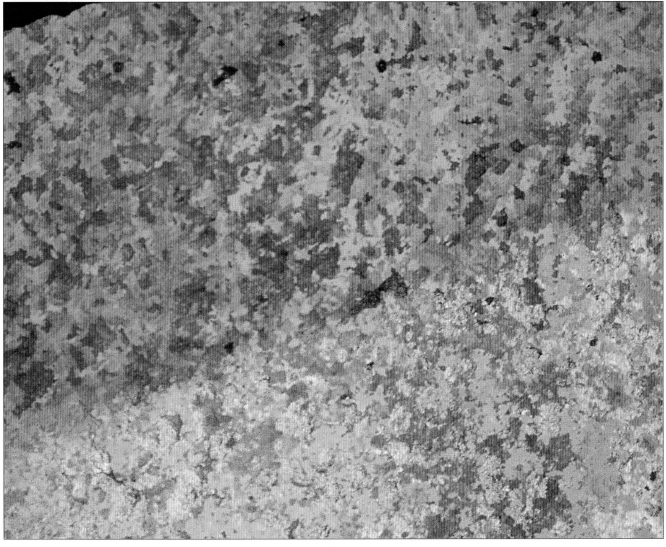

CARIBBEAN

Personal Experiences
Shoemaker Leon
Compere-Leandre. One
of only four known sur-
vivors of the 8 May 1902
eruption of Mont Pelée,
Martinique.
*On May 8th, at about eight
o'clock in the morning, I was
seated on the doorstep of my
house, which was in the*

'Mont Pelée is no more to be feared by St. Pierre than Vesuvius is feared by Naples. We confess we cannot understand this panic. Where could one be better off than St. Pierre?'. Designed to reduce growing desperation amongst the 30,000 inhabitants of the bustling French colonial town on the island of Martinique, these words in the local paper, *Les Colonies* now stand as an ironic and poignant epitaph to the worst volcanic disaster in the Caribbean. Less than 48 hours later, St. Pierre — the 'Paris of the West Indies' — was wiped from the face of the Earth, and all but four of its inhabitants (see Personal Experience on this page) roasted to death in a matter of two or three minutes.

For most of the time since first French settlers reached the island in 1653, the Mont Pelée volcano — also known as the Bald

VIRGIN ISLANDS

CARRIBEAN

SABA

SOUFRIERE HILLS
MONTSERRAT

SOUFRIÉRE AND
(GUADELOUPE)

GUADELOUPE

LESSER ANTILLES

DOMINIICA

MT PÉLEE

MARTINIQUE

ST LUCIA

SOUFRIERE (ST.VINCENT)

BARBADOS

KICK-'EM JENNY

GRENADA

TOBAGO

TRINIDAD

Mountain — had slumbered, waking irritably on two occasions, in 1792 and 1851, to let loose some desultory rumbles and sprinkle a little ash on the fortunate inhabitants of this tropical paradise. Little concern was expressed during April 1902, therefore, when new steaming fumaroles, sulphurous smells, and some minor trembling of the ground indicated that Pelée was beginning to stir once more. Fear and panic resulting from the appearance of a fresh, bubbling cone in an old dried-up crater lake — the L'Etang Sec — falling ash, which coated everything and everyone in the town, and an increasingly strong stench of sulphur, was alleviated to some extent by the report of a scientific commision appointed by the French governor, which recognised 'no immediate danger and no reason for abandoning the city'. In fact the population of St. Pierre actually grew as a combination of a forthcoming election, and the perception that the town would provide more protection should the volcano erupt, drew in more people from the surrounding countryside.

By early May, however, the population was clearly on the edge of panic, fostered by portentious plagues of venomenous ants, centipedes, and snakes seeking refuge from the increasingly violent activity, and the hellish fates of sugar mill workers boiled to death and entombed by a river of scalding mud which burst from the now lake-filled L'Etang Sec on 5 May.

The gloriously sunny morning of 7 May was not to last, and for the residents of St. Pierre, time itself would cease at 07.52 as they were obliterated by a gigantic volcanic explosion directed at the town like the blast from a shotgun. Driven by the enormous pressures of expanding volcanic gases, a glowing cloud of molten fragments and superheated steam flowed down the flanks of Pelée, battering the town with hurricane force, flattening buildings in sec-

VOLCANO LOG: THE CARIBBEAN
Active volcanoes and volcanic fields: 17

The biggest and the deadliest

VOLCANO	ERUPTION	VOL (cu km) ERUPTED	CASUALTIES
La Soufrière (St. Vincent)	1812	0.1	Several **MA**
Mont Pelée (Martinique)	1902	0.1	31,000 **PM**
La Soufrière (St. Vincent)	1902	0.1	2,000 **P**
La Soufrière (Guadeloupe)	1976	0.0001	—
La Soufrière (St. Vincent)	1979	0.01	—
Soufriere Hills (Montserrat)	1995	0.1	—

Key: **A**=ash fall and/or falling blocks **D**=disease **F**=famine **G**=gases **L**=landslides **La**=lavas **M**=mudflows **P**=pyroclastic flows **T**=tsunami

southeast part of the town. All of a sudden I felt a terrible wind blowing, the Earth began to tremble, and the sky suddenly became dark. I turned to go into the house, made with great difficulty the three or four steps that separated me from my room, and felt my arms and legs burning, also my body. I dropped upon a table. At this moment, four others sought refuge in my room, crying and writhing with pain, although their garments showed no sign of having been touched by flame. At the end of 10 minutes one of these, the young Delavaud girl, aged 10 fell dead; the others left. I then got up and went into another room, where I found the father Delavaud, still clothed and lying on the bed, dead. He was purple and inflated, but the clothing was intact. I went out and found in the court two corpses interlocked; they were the bodies of the two young men who had been with me in the room. Re-entering the house, I came upon the bodies of two men who had been in the garden when I returned to my house at the beginning of the catastrophe. Crazed and almost overcome, I threw myself upon a bed, inert and awaiting death.

CARIBBEAN

Personal Experiences
Volcanologist Bill McGuire on the 17 September explosive eruption of the Soufriere Hills volcano, Montserrat.

On the night of 17 September 1996 the volcano really blew its top. While enjoying a final nightcap before turning in, I suddenly became aware that things were getting noisy outside, a combination of dogs barking, thunder and lightning, and a rumbling, whooshing sound rather like a distant jet engine. The volcano had 'gone explosive', and the volcano observatory was in a similar state. All the seismographs were going wild, indicating that something much bigger than usual was going on, and the entire scientific staff of the observatory milled about in the single, small command centre as they tried to build up a picture of what was happening. Overhead we could make out a huge, towering dark cloud, shot through with near-continuous threads of lightning, against a rapidly disappearing background of stars. There was a red glow on the eastern horizon, in the direction of the Tar River, and reports from towns in the east of falling rocks and buildings on fire.

RIGHT: Sulphur Springs at Qualibou on St Lucia. The bubbling, steaming craters last erupted in 1766.

onds, ripping cannons from their mountings, and contemptuously hurling a three ton statue of the Virgin Mary a distance of 20m (65ft). The flesh of some 29,000 human beings was instantly boiled, with the vapourisation of body fluids causing organs to explode and skull sutures to pop apart. At the same time, however, clothing was often untouched, indicating that the passage of the scalding blast was so rapid that there was insufficient time for clothing to ignite. The immolating hurricane continued into the harbour where it swept across the surface of the sea annihilating 15 ships and their crews, and crippling the remaining two. Minutes later the destruction was complete and the lifeless remains of St. Pierre blazed from end to end.

The *nuée ardente* (literally 'glowing cloud'), or what volcanologists call apyroclastic flow, which erased St. Pierre, is the most terrible and feared of all eruptive phenomena, and one which characterises the activity of many of the 16 volcanoes forming the arc of Caribbean islands known as the Lesser Antilles. By an extraordinary coincidence, in fact, a mere 24 hours before the Martinique disaster a similarly lethal pyroclastic flow eruption of the La Soufrière volcano took another 1,700 lives on the neighbouring island of St. Vincent. News of this event, reaching St. Pierre on the evening of the seventh, actually went someway towards reassuring the population as they took to their beds, mistakenly believing that the St. Vincent blast would relieve the building pressures beneath their own volcano. It might be expected that close to 31,000 deaths in a matter of days, and the continued generation of further *nuées*, would ensure evacuation of the slopes around Pelée. Sadly, this was not to be, and a further 2,000 lives were lost on 30 August, including the inhabitants of Morne Rouge who, only 114 days earlier, had observed the death throes of St. Pierre.

Apart from the disastrous events of 1902, few destructive eruptions are known from the Lesser Antilles, although the historical record only goes back to the 1630s when the first European settlers became established on the islands. Since the first recorded eruption of La Soufrière on the French island of Guadeloupe in 1690, only around 33 eruptions have taken place at the regions 17 active volcanoes, the great majority of these at Mont Pelée and at the Soufrières of St. Vincent and Guadeloupe. Somewhat surprisingly, however, the most active Caribbean volcano of this century is not even visible. The enigmatically-named submarine volcano — Kick 'em Jenny — has erupted 10 times since the start of World War II, and twice in the last nine years. Worryingly, for the inhabitants of nearby Grenada, Kick 'em Jenny is an unstable volcano which is prone to collapse, and scientists have recently been concerned at the resulting potential tsunami threat.

CARIBBEAN

ABOVE and OPPOSITE: After nearly 350 years of quiescence, Soufriere Hills volcano on Montserrat reawakened in 1995 with the extrusion of a lava dome that had grown more than 100m (328ft) thick within a year. Collapses of this dome triggered pyroclastic flows that entered the sea.

On 17 September 1996, a short explosive eruption spewed out lava blocks large enough to force the inward collapse of roofs of buildings over a kilometre distant (ABOVE).

ABOVE RIGHT: Only steam emission shows that an active lava dome is present inside the crater of Soufriere Hills, Montserrat. As the dome grows, it exerts pressure on the old crater walls, raising fears of a possible landslide.

Unlike the runny lavas that characterise eruptions at oceanic volcanoes, such as Hawaii and Iceland, those of the Lesser Antilles volcanoes — where Atlantic Ocean floor is being subducted beneath the Caribbean Plate — are glutinous and slow moving. Consequently, they rarely form flows, but instead pile up over the eruptive vent to form huge and typically unstable domes. Often, gigantic spines of sticky lava are pushed skyward from the surface of a lava dome, before collapsing and disintigrating to form pyroclastic flows. Such a spine rose from a lava dome which formed in the crater of Pelée during the months following the destruction of St. Pierre, rising like a huge tombstone to a height of 300m (985ft), before finally crumbling away through 1903 and 1904. The enormous power of the 8 May blast itself resulted, in fact, from the accumulation of fresh, gassy magma beneath an older, solidified dome which sealed the vent. When the pressures became critical, the frothy new magma burst forth like a cork from a champagne bottle; a bottle aimed precisely at St. Pierre.

Lava domes and pyroclastic flows are once again big news in the Caribbean, ever since the dormant Soufriere Hills volcano on the 'Emerald Isle' of Montserrat awakened in July 1995. After over 350 years of peace, the first rumblings beneath the Soufriere Hills took the form of a 'swarm' of earthquakes during the final years of the 18th century. Similar rumblings during the 1930s and 1960s suggested that fresh magma was on its way to the surface, so volcanologists were not surprised when the volcano at last burst into life.

The early activity consisted of spectacular rather than particularly dangerous steam blasts as the rising magma came into contact with sub-surface water. Within months, however, sticky magma oozed out of a vent at the summit and began to build a giant lava dome which collapsed periodically to form pyroclastic flows and falling ash on the flanks of the volcano. With conditions becoming increasingly difficult for the inhabitants of this beautiful but tiny island, the southern half of the island, including the capital and only major town, Plymouth, was evacuated, and the 12,000 population halved as many sought refuge on neighbouring islands and in the United Kingdom, of which Montserrat is a dependent territory.

Throughout the summer of 1996, the lava dome continued to increase in size, until on the morning of 17 September, a major episode of collapse triggered a spectacular series of pyroclastic flows which travelled down the Tar River valley on the opposite side of the volcano from Plymouth. Clouds of ash rising from the pyroclastic flows were carried across the island by the prevailing winds and dumped on the capital. Further collapses late that night reduced the weight of the dome and, just before midnight, allowed gassy magma trapped beneath the dome to burst eastward in a directed explosion

CARIBBEAN

BELOW: *After the eruption of 17 September 1996, much of the active lava dome at Soufriere Hills had been blasted away, sending out pyroclastic flows.*

RIGHT: Columns of hot ash rise above a pyroclastic flow racing down the Tar River Valley on Montserrat. The ashes, buoyed up by hot air, were transported westward by the prevailing wind, falling on the opposite side of the island.

OVERLEAF: A new lava dome emerged through the crater lake at the Soufriere of St. Vincent in 1979. The eruption gave observers a unique opportunity to study the growth of a lava dome.

(see Personal Experience page 126). The village of Long Ground was directly in the firing line, and a number of inhabitants who had refused to leave the area despite the dangers found themselves on the receiving end of a frightening bombardment of hot lumps of dome rock. Over 50 percent of the buildings were damaged, and the area peppered with impact craters up to 5m (16ft) across. Miraculously, however, no one was killed or injured.

As if the explosions were not enough, a great column of ash and pumice rose 14km (9 miles) into the atmosphere, showering the entire southern half of the island and causing major problems for an Air Canada jet which unknowingly flew into the cloud. Again, however, there were no casualties, although for safety a further 2,000 people were temporarily evacuated to locations further north, and the volcano calmed down after less than an hour. So far the activity at the Soufriere Hills volcano has taken no lives, but although no further explosive eruptions have occurred, the dome continues to grow, and at the time of writing (March 1997) was twice as big as before 17 September 1996. The remaining Montserratians continue to pray that worse is not to come, and the scientists at the Volcano Observatory monitor activity around the clock. Ninety-five years on, no one wants another St. Pierre.

VOLCANIC
ISLANDS

Personal Experiences
Bory de Saint-Vincent describes the destruction of the town of Guarachico during the 1706 eruption of Teide, Tenerife.
Guarrachico was a pleasant town, surrounded with fertile fields and rich vineyards; it

Iceland is a strangely misleading name for a country built entirely of lava; perhaps Fireland would have been a more appropriate epithet, and one which may, indeed, have been adopted by the earliest nordic settlers had one of the islands many active volcanoes, such as Hekla, Krafla, Askja, or Grimsvötn, been erupting when they first set foot in this bleak but beautiful land.

Straddling the Mid-Atlantic Ridge, where masses of fresh magma fill the space left as the European and North American plates creep apart by a few centimetres a year, Iceland is one of the most volcanically-active places on Earth. The island and the

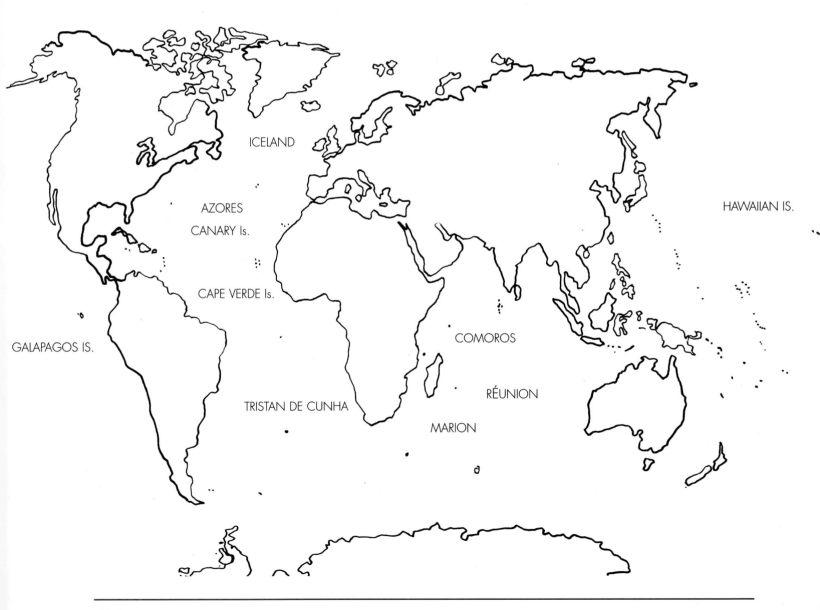

ICELAND

AZORES

CANARY Is.

CAPE VERDE Is.

HAWAIIAN IS.

GALAPAGOS IS.

COMOROS

RÉUNION

TRISTAN DE CUNHA

MARION

surrounding sea constitute one of the planet's volcanic breeding grounds, where brand new volcanoes can burst onto the scene with little warning, but with much accompanying mayhem.

Such a birth was recorded on 23 January 1973, when the 5,000 townsfolk of Vestmannaeyjar, on the tiny island of Heimaey off the south coast of Iceland, awoke to find that a new volcano had exploded onto the scene at the edge of town. Despite their homes being progressively buried in cinders, the islanders battled for months to try and prevent lava flows from damming the harbour of Iceland's main fishing port, spraying the flows with millions of gallons of seawater in an attempt to slow them down. When the eruption ended six months later, it proved —in fact — to have been a blessing in disguise, with the new lava flows forming a more sheltered harbour, and providing a source of heating for the local hospital.

Ten years earlier, on 14 November 1963 an even more spectacular volcanic birth occurred when fishing boat cook, Olafur

VOLCANO LOG: OCEANIC AND ISLANDS
Active volcanoes and volcanic fields

Arctic Ocean	2
Azores (NE Atlantic)	12
Canary Islands (E Atlantic)	6
Cape Verde Islands (E Atlantic)	4
East and South Pacific	11
Hawaii (Pacific)	10
Iceland	33
Indian Ocean	15
Other Atlantic	13
Total	106

The biggest and the deadliest

VOLCANO	ERUPTION	VOL (cu km) ERUPTED	CASUALTIES
Askja (Iceland)	1875	0.1	—
Fogo (Cape Verde Islands)	1995	0.01	—
Furnas (Azores)	1630	0.2	>200 M
Heimaey (Iceland)	1973	0.2	—
Hekla (Iceland)	1300	0.2	600 F
Katla (Iceland)	1311	0.1	many Fl
Krafla (Iceland)	1984	0.1	—
Laki (Iceland)	1783	10	9,350 Fl
Lanzarote (Canary Islands)	1730	1	few
Surtsey (Iceland)	1963	1	—

Key: **A**=ash fall and/or falling blocks **F**=Famine **Fl**=floods **G**=gases **L**=landslides **La**=lavas **M**=mudflows **P**=pyroclastic flows **T**=tsunami

had besides, a very good and commodius port. During the night of 5 May 1706, a noise was heard underground like that of a storm, and the sea retreated. When the day broke, and rendered visible the phenomenon, the peak was seen covered with a fearful red vapour. The air was on fire, a sulphurous smell suffocated the frightened animals. The waters were covered with steam similar to that over the boiling springs; all at once the Earth moved and opened; torrents of lava flowed from the crater of Teide, and rushed into the plains from the northwest. The town, half swallowed up in the clefts in the ground, half buried by the vomited lava, disappeared entirely. The sea, returning to its bed, inundated the ruins of the port, which had sunk down; waves and heaps of cinders occupy the site of Guarrachico. The inhabitants tried to save themselves by immediate flight, but most of them made futile attempts; some were swallowed up in the clefts, buried alive; others, suffocated by the sulphurous vapours, fell asphyxiated in their attempts to escape. Many of these unfortunates, however, escaped with much peril, and seeing from far their homes in flames, flattered themselves with the hope that they had escaped, when nearly all were crushed by a hail of enormous stones, the last effect of the eruption.

Personal Experiences

Only rarely are the first moments of a volcanic eruption recorded. The late Gordon Macdonald, was lucky enough to be perfectly placed for the start of the 1955 eruption of Kilauea on Hawaii. *First, hairline cracks opened in the ground, gradually widening to two or three inches. Then from the crack there poured out a cloud of white choking sulphur fume. This was followed a few minutes later by the ejection of scattered tiny fragments of red-hot lava, and then the appearance at the surface of a small bulb of viscous molten lava. The bulb gradually swelled to a diameter of 1 to 1.5 feet [30–45cm], and started to spread laterally to form a lava flow. From the top of the bulb there developed a fountain of molten lava which gradually built around itself a cone of solidified spatter.*

ABOVE RIGHT: On Hawaii slow extrusion of lava produces smooth-surfaced pahoehoe flows. The surfaces can become corrugated by the motion of lava beneath. When small tongues ooze through the surface, their combined texture is described graphically as entrail pahoehoe.

BELOW RIGHT: The Puu Oo lava lake on Hawaii. The surface of the lake rapidly cools to form a thin crust that gets broken into plates by currents in the lava beneath.

Vestmann, spotted a column of dark smoke on the horizon. Assuming that a ship was on fire, the fishermen went to investigate, only to find that a new volcano had grown unnoticed on the sea bed and was about to break the surface to form a new island — Surtsey, named after Surtur, the mythical giant of fire. With magma and sea-water able to mix freely, violent explosions were nearly continuous, hurling steaming and whistling volcanic bombs over a kilometre from the vent. Four days later, the baby volcano was over half a kilo-metre (a third of a mile) long and nearly 50m (160ft) high, and still erupting strongly sending a column of ash to height of 9km (6 miles) or more. After five months of activity, the island had an area of over 2sq km (0,75sq miles), and a widespread capping of fresh lavas protected the loose ash and cinders from the continuous pounding of the Atlantic waves. Ash and lavas continued to be erupted for the next three years until things finally quietened down in June 1967. Since then the island has turned from a natural geo-logical laboratory to a biological one, as scientists make the most of a unique opportunity to observe how pristine land — even such a tiny speck in the hostile, wind-lashed north Atlantic — is colonised by life.

In all, just over a hundred oceanic volcanoes, have managed to grow, like Surtsey — and Iceland itself — large enough to penetrate the surface of the sea and form islands, but many thousands more remain hidden beneath the waves. Some of the island volcanoes, such as the Azores, Ascension, and Tristan da Cunha, in the Atlantic, and St. Paul in the Indian Ocean, lie either on or close to the network of mid-ocean ridges where new ocean floor is being formed and where the Earth's plates are moving apart. Others, such as Hawaii and Pitcairn in the Pacific, are far from any plate margin, and sit above 'hot spots' in the Earth's crust where plumes of magma rise from deep within the interior of the planet.

In contrast to the explosive behaviour of subduction-zone vol-canoes, such as Krakatoa, Mont Pelée, and Mount St. Helens, ocean island volcanoes are generally characterised by the relatively quiet extrusion of fluid basaltic lavas, although more violent activity can and does occur, particularly in the Azores, Canary, and Cape Verde archipelagoes of the northeast Atlantic. At times, enormous volumes of runny, basalt lava can be erupted very rapidly, during what are called basaltic flood eruptions. The geological record provides evi-dence of some gigantic floods of basaltic lava, including those of the northwest United States. Here, a single flow field of the Columbia River flood basalt covers an area of 40,000sq km (15,500sq miles) and may have been erupted in only a few weeks. The only basaltic flood eruption witnessed during historic times was considerably smaller. Nevertheless, the Laki fissure eruption (also known as the

VOLCANIC
ISLANDS

RIGHT: The surfaces of pahoehoe lavas often solidify quickly enough to form roofs and maintain the lava interior at high temperature. Skylights occur where the roof locally breaks, allowing observers to measure the velocity and temperature of the lava beneath.

BELOW: Tongues of lava enter the sea off Hawaii's Kilauea volcano. The lava temperature sets the ocean boiling.

ABOVE: Vigorous lava fountains playing along fissures that fed a 23km (14 miles) long lava flow on Mauna Loa in 1984.

LEFT: The Pu'u 'O'o lava lake on Hawaii. The chilled lava surface (on the right) appears brighter than the solidified lava which had earlier overflowed the lake's margins.

VOLCANIC
ISLANDS

Skaftar Fires) which occurred in Iceland during 1783, still represented one of the greatest disasters to hit the island since it was settled. On 8 June lava poured from a 24km (15 mile) long series of fissures, preceded by the ejection of great clouds of ash. Five months later, when the eruption finally ended, the lavas had buried over 500sq km (200sq miles) of southern Iceland, along with several farms. Ash, generated by violent explosions as the rising magma came into contact with ground- and surface-water, fell as far away as Norway and Scotland, and a dry, sulphurous haze settled over the whole country. As crops shrivelled under the cloud, and livestock sickened and died through eating contaminated fodder, famine reigned across the land, and over 25 percent of the island's population starved to death in the following years. Just over 50 years earlier, a similar huge outpouring of highly fluid basaltic lava devastated large areas of the Canary Island of Lanzarote, producing one of the largest lava flows of historic times. Between 1730 and 1736 lava and ash continued to burst from a giant fissure system, eventually covering over 200sq km (77sq miles) — almost a quarter — of the island, destroying towns and villages, and turning fertile farmland into a volcanic desert.

ABOVE LEFT: Rugged pahoehoe lava on Fernandina, one of the Galapagos Islands.

BELOW LEFT: Morning mists rising over the Cumbre Vieja volcano on La Palma, Canary Islands.

RIGHT: El Teide, on Tenerife, stands 3,710m (12,169ft) above sea level and is officially the highest point in Spain. It last had a summit eruption several thousand years ago. Historical eruptions on the island have occurred at lower altitudes, many effusing lava flows that threatened coastal towns and villages.

CENTER RIGHT: Piton de la Fournaise on the Indian Ocean island of Réunion is one of the world's most active volcanoes. Activity is normally effusive and characterised by the quiet extrusion of basaltic lava flows. La Fournaise has erupted 75 times over the past 100 years, the last time being in 1992.

BELOW RIGHT: Strombolian explosions during the 1971 eruption of Teneguia (La Palma), the most recent volcanic activity in the Canary Islands.

VOLCANIC
ISLANDS

The generally quiet eruption of basaltic lavas also characterises the volcanoes of the Hawaiian Islands in the Pacific and the island of Réunion in the Indian Ocean, which host some of the most active volcanoes in the world. The Hawaiian volcano, Kilauea, was almost continually active for most of the 19th century, and the Pu'u 'O'o vent has been erupting almost continuously since early 1983. Similarly, Piton de la Fournaise on Réunion is a particularly dynamic volcano which has erupted 75 times over the last 100 years. The Hawaiian Island volcanoes are the biggest on Earth, with Mauna Loa on Big Island rising from the sea floor to over 4,000m (13,000ft) above sea level, a total height of 9,000m (29,500ft), and having a volume of 40,000cu km (52 million cu yd). The gently-sloping forms of these huge volcanoes contrast sharply with the steep flanks of other oceanic volcanoes such as the Cumbre Vieja on La Palma and Teide on Tenerife, both in the Canary Islands.

As they get bigger and bigger, however, both types of volcano become unstable, and large chunks fall off them into the adjacent oceans creating tsunami; giant waves with the potential to devastate coastlines thousands of kilometres away. Some of the Hawaiian landslides are over 1,000cu km (1.3 million cu yd) in volume, and

the last collapse, around 100,000 years ago, produced one of biggest waves ever known. Three hundred metres (1,000ft) high when it hit the local islands, there is evidence that the wave was still immensely destructive even when it reached the coast of Australia. Such an event occurring today would be catastrophic for those living around the Pacific Rim. There would be little time to escape as such huge waves travel at speeds of several hundred kilometres per hour. Nor is the Atlantic safe. During the last eruption but one, in 1949, part of the very steep western flank of the Cumbre Vieja volcano on the island of La Palma in the Canary Islands, started to slide seaward. Fortunately the movement stopped after a few metres, but sometime in the future — perhaps not many years hence — a new eruption will finish the job, and up to 100sq km (130,000sq yd) of rock will fall into the North Atlantic. Estimates for the size of the consequent tsunami when it hits the eastern United States range as high as 200m (650ft)! Further south, off the west coast of Africa, the giant, unstable, Fogo volcano in the Cape Verde Islands poses a similar threat, this time to the Canary Islands themselves and to the Atlantic coastline of Europe.